International Cooperation and Public Goods

International Cooperation and Public Goods

Opportunities for the Western Alliance

Mark A. Boyer

The Johns Hopkins University Press

Baltimore and London

The Johns Hopkins University Press
2715 North Charles Street
Baltimore, Maryland 21218-4139
The Johns Hopkins Press Ltd., London

Library of Congress Cataloging-in-Publication Data

Boyer, Mark A.
    International cooperation and public goods : opportunities for the
Western alliance / Mark A. Boyer.
        p.   cm.
    Includes bibliographical references and index.
    ISBN 0-8018-4440-1
    1. Security, International. 2. International cooperation.
3. Public goods. 4. International relations. 5. International
economic relations. 6. North Atlantic Treaty Organization.
I. Title.
JX1952.B7244   1992
355′.031′091821—dc20   92-14737

A catalog record for this book is available from the British Library

To Sondra

Contents

Figures

Tables

Preface

The research that follows takes on a number of tasks. First, at a substantive level, it questions the conventional wisdom about the nature of Western alliance burden sharing and presents, I hope, a more complete picture of the contributions made to enhance alliance security. Second, it examines the burden sharing issue from a broader security policy framework that goes beyond conceptualizing security as synonymous with military defense. Last, and possibly most important from my own perspective, this book presents an argument about why nations can and will cooperate in pursuit of common goals. In this way, the book is primarily a theoretical critique and expansion of earlier work in the theory of public goods. Although only Western alliance security cooperation is examined in the book, the theoretical constructs developed here are applicable to other international relations situations and also to other generic public goods problems.

In terms of completing this book and getting started in academia more generally, I have many people to thank. Davis Bobrow and Jon Wilkenfeld provided me with a great deal of guidance and help during and since my years at the University of Maryland. I was very fortunate to be able to capitalize on their abilities and to develop working relationships and friendships with both of them. Joe Oppenheimer was instrumental in my training and intellectual growth, as well. His enthusiasm and drive as a teacher were inspiring and I hope that I carry some of that same energy into my own classrooms. Moreover, particularly when it comes to the more formal aspects of the theory of this book, I owe a great debt to Joe for the hours we spent around his kitchen table and also for an intense working session in Storrs. I am also thankful for close contact with Catherine Kelleher (from whom my European focus largely stems), Martin McGuire, and George Quester. I cannot compliment enough the security studies program they have built at Maryland.

At the University of Connecticut, I found a working environment no less stimulating and supportive. Betty Hanson has been the best colleague one could ask for, expecially for anyone starting out in academia. Her input on the revisions of the manuscript has been invaluable. Larry Bowman has been an extremely supportive chairman, and I am glad for the opportunity to work with him and to become friends during these past few years. Larry has truly succeeded in building a congenial place for young scholars to get on their feet in the discipline. His reading of chapter 1 was crucial to its formulation and readability.

Others I would like to thank for their help on this project—reading some or all of the manuscript or helping with particular problems—include Polly Allen, Margaret Conway, Karen Donfried, Bart Kaminski, Keith Hartley, Martin Heisler, Helene Holm-Pedersen, David Hubert, Rodger Payne, John Rourke, Matt Rubiner, Bruce Russett, Todd Sandler, Glenn Snyder, Bram Treistram, Imanuel Wexler, and David Wightman. The research assistance of David Hubert and Deirdre Allison was invaluable.

I was fortunate to obtain generous institutional support. The award of a two-year SSRC-MacArthur Fellowship in International Peace and Security allowed me the freedom to focus exclusively on my graduate studies during my last years at Maryland. The University of Connecticut Research Foundation granted me a junior faculty summer fellowship and also a small faculty research grant, which were instrumental in completing the project. I also thank Everett Ladd for opening the archives of the Roper Center for Public Opinion Research to me; that resource was extremely useful for the material required for chapter 4. The Gallup International Research Institute in London cordially allowed me to pick through its files in March 1989. A trip to Berlin in October 1990 for a seminar for junior academics sponsored by NATO and the Paul Loebe Institute and a similar trip to Japan sponsored by the Japanese Ministry of Foreign Affairs gave a real-world perspective to the theoretical world I got lost in at times during my research and writing. Both trips provided insights into the problems I was working with that could only be obtained from being there and talking to policymakers and other academics outside the United States.

I also want to thank a number of other people and journals for granting me permission to use portions of previously published material. Much of appendix A and parts of other chapters were published as "Trading Public Goods in the Western Alliance System," *Journal of Conflict Resolution* 33 (1989):700–27. I thank Bruce Russett and Sage Publications for allowing me to use that material here. Much of chapter 3 and some of chapter 5 appeared as "A Simple and Untraditional Analysis of Western Alliance Burden-Sharing," *Defence Economics* 1 (1990):243–59. I thank Todd Sandler, Keith Hartley, and Harwood Academic Publishers for permission to use those pieces. Herbert Kiesling allowed me to use a number of figures from his public goods trading model, Urban Institute working paper, 1972; they appear in appendix B. Mancur Olson and Richard Zeckhauser and the *Review of Economics and Statistics* graciously granted me permission to use in chapter 2 three figures from their 1966 article "An Economic Theory of Alliances." And some of the public opinion data in chapter 4 is used with the permission of Philip Hastings and was taken from various volumes of the *Index to International Public Opinion* (Greenwood Press).

This book would also never have come together without the efforts of several people at Johns Hopkins University Press. Henry Tom stuck with me throughout and gave me a better understanding of the process. The work of Barbara Lamb, Heather Peterson, and Diane Hammond is also much appreciated.

And last, but not least, I want to thank my family, Sondra, Craig, and Dana, for the love, support, fun, and craziness they have provided me through the years. Sondra was not only a spectator in this project but was also a cheerful—and incredibly accurate—data coder. We make a great team. I dedicate this book to her. I also wish to express my love and thanks to my parents, Ralph and Marian Boyer, for their support of my decisions through the years, even when they may not have thought them wise. They taught me to take on challenges.

Before closing, I want to pay special tribute to Dick Flickinger and Gerry Hudson, both of Wittenberg University. Both are first-rate teachers and scholars who stimulated my interest in international relations and helped point me in the right professional direction. If not for knowing them, I probably would have ended up a lawyer. I want to thank them both for saving me from that fate.

International Cooperation
and Public Goods

1

International Security and the Theory of Public Goods

THE WORDS *alliance* and *security* conjure up images of military policy. It is not surprising, then, that research focusing on these two terms centers on their military dimensions. But in contemporary international affairs, security is not a one-dimensional concept, and nations define security across economic, military, political, environmental, and even social dimensions. Studying alliances and security policies by examining only the military leaves one with, at best, an incomplete picture of the security strategies adopted and implemented by nations and, at worst, a picture that is misleading intellectually and inflames international relationships. Thus any effort to build theories of alliances or international cooperation or to evaluate the success or failure of cooperation in a particular international situation must account for the interplay of issue areas often thought to be isolated from one another.

Theories of International Cooperation and the Real World

Underlying this study's search for a new theory of international cooperation is the assumption that national security is maintained through the cultivation of diverse policy instruments, ranging from military defense to foreign aid to international monetary cooperation and beyond. In earlier times, high politics, or political-military affairs, was synonymous with national security policy, and low politics, or economic affairs, was a secondary concern. But as national economies became increasingly sensitive to the influence of external political and economic occurrences, low politics was thrust into a policy arena once occupied only by military defense issues.

3

In the 1970s, economics came to the fore of international relations. The confluence of developments—such as the evolution of the economic system from the establishment of the Bretton Woods system to its collapse, the rise of resource cartels, and Soviet attainment of military parity with the United States—made it necessary for Western security strategy to be formulated on many levels to harmonize the requirements of military defense with economic stability and prosperity.

In a work exploring these new trends in national security policies, Klaus Knorr stated that "national security concerns arise when vital national values (i.e., core values) are perceived as being threatened by adverse foreign actions or events" (1977:8). He went on to suggest that values outside the military security realm had become vulnerable to external influences as interdependence among nations increased. This rise of nonmilitary security concerns has taken on special meaning for the advanced industrialized countries, where sensitivity to interdependence has been particularly acute, because of the success of the liberal economic order and because past security strategies did not address issues of economic or political security in the traditional power politics environment.

Certainly, the interplay of these policy areas was important in the public sector prior to the 1970s, as illustrated by Cordell Hull's statement that "unhampered trade dovetail[s] with peace; high tariffs trade barriers, and unfair economic competition, with war" (Cooper, 1987:299). But one-dimensional security studies have failed to factor economic and political affairs into their analyses ever since the 1970s.

More appropriately, analysts must recognize that nations in the contemporary international system cultivate a mix of policies designed to serve multidimensional security objectives. This means pursuing monetary and fiscal policies that promote economic stability and growth, military policies that preserve physical survival and do not detract from the pursuit of other national security objectives, trade policies that ensure access to foreign markets, and foreign aid policies that promote economic development and stability for foreign economic commitments. Examples of these realities can be seen in the world events of the 1980s: the debate over massive cuts in the American defense budget in response to budgetary pressure and changes in the military threat; the Soviet Union's adoption of *glasnost* and *perestroika* in an effort to deal with a sluggish, backward economic system; and the Eastern European states' dismantling of the political structures that directly tied them to the Soviet security system. All of these policies aimed to enhance individual, national, and collective security.

Additionally, comparing the conceptions of security held by various industrialized countries substantiates the value placed on nonmilitary security concerns. The Japanese conception of comprehensive security shows that military spending is not the only measure, or even the most important one, for Japanese national and alliance security policies. Japanese security concerns include a range of policies, from development assistance to trade policy to resource supply security (Chapman, Drifte, Gow, 1982; Bobrow, 1984; Yasatumo, 1986). Western European efforts to secure stable energy supplies by cooperating with the U.S.S.R. in building a gas pipeline during the 1980s also reflect security strategies that include more than military concerns. Other more general studies of contemporary security concerns by Richard Ullman (1983), Lester Brown (1977), and Jessica Mathews (1989) have identified security threats originating from environmental and demographic pressures, resource supply concerns, and Third World political-economic turmoil, to name only a few.

In addition, a satisfactory level of security cannot be achieved individually in a world of accelerating interdependence. In such a world, "the distinction between domestic and foreign issues becomes blurred" (Keohane and Nye, 1977:25), and policy must account for this reality if a nation is to remain secure. Examples of such blurred borders abound. Tight money policy, military buildup, and high interest rates in the United States resulted in foreign capital flows to the United States and high interest rates abroad; the refusal of the Bundesbank to expand the West German money supply perpetuated the fall of the dollar in foreign exchange markets; decisions by Western European countries and Japan to purchase natural gas from the U.S.S.R. resulted in technology transfer restrictions by the United States. Each of these is evidence of the need for multinational policy coordination and collective action.

In spite of these realities, studies of alliances have focused on military affairs alone, and studies of international cooperation have limited their scope to a single issue area (e.g. Oye, 1986; Keohane, 1984). Although policymakers have, at least rhetorically, acknowledged that national security is influenced by both military and nonmilitary forces, international relations scholars have failed to integrate these forces into a general approach to alliances, security studies, and international cooperation. Few attempts have been made to integrate these issue areas into a macrolevel theory of security cooperation that can explain cooperation and conflict among nations pursuing common security interests. Many scholars have acknowledged the varied facets of national security in contemporary international relations, but few have provided a foundation for the study of security cooperation across issue areas. Others have developed useful concepts for the study of international cooperation but have not applied them beyond the one-dimensional policy setting.

Based on public goods theory, the work that follows uses an integrated approach to the analysis of international cooperation. In contrast to earlier, narrower studies, this work yields significantly different results regarding (1) the optimality of public good provision in collective action situations, (2) the potential for and the value of policy linkages across issue areas, (3) the nature of alliance burden sharing, and (4) the future of cooperation among the Western alliance nations in the face of a changing international political-military environment.

Using the Western alliance system,[1] I show that international cooperation can take the form of policy specialization by individual nations, based on considerations of political and economic comparative advantage as found in international trade theory. For instance, one nation may be able to produce military defense for an alliance more efficiently than another nation can, while the other nation is able to put its foreign aid expenditures to better use than the first. If each dimension of alliance contribution were evaluated in isolation from the others, free riding would be apparent and expected, because not all nations would specialize in any one dimension. Taken together, however, these disproportionate burdens are really tradeoffs. For example, the American military buildup in the 1980s can be compared to the simultaneous Japanese and West German efforts to stabilize the value of the dollar and to help the United States adjust its external economic accounts.

This book analyzes the conventional wisdom regarding the Western alliance, examines its theoretical base, and revises the hypotheses of public goods theory. It first focuses on the theoretical underpinnings of earlier studies of international cooperation and then empirically examines the broader nature of Western alliance security. The remainder of this chapter lays out a number of other conceptual points necessary for an understanding of the work that lies ahead.

International Relations and the Theory of Public Goods

Efficiency and equity in the provision of societal needs and wants have long been central concerns of the social sciences, especially for scholars of political science and economics. Social scientists are continually searching for evaluations of the efficiency of society's utilization of its political and economic resources and evaluations of the equity of the distribution of those resources. Any daily newspaper, however, makes it clear that these evaluations most often yield negative results.

Anyone familiar with Mancur Olson's classic work, *The Logic of*

Collective Action, should not be surprised by such results. Olson stated the problem as follows:

> Groups of individuals with common interests are expected to act on behalf of their common interests much as single individuals are often expected to act on behalf of their personal interests. . . . [However], unless the number of individuals in a group is quite small, or unless there is coercion or some other special device to make individuals act in their common interest, rational, self-interested individuals will not act to achieve their common or group interests. (1965: 1–2)

At the heart of this problem lies the nature of the goods that are desired by groups of individuals. For goods that are private in nature—that is, goods that can be consumed by only one individual—efficient solutions to resource allocation problems are easily found. Regardless of whether a private good is an apple or an aspirin, the good is consumed by only one individual, and the value of the production is given by its price in terms of either money or another private good.[2]

In Olson's problem, though, and seemingly in many situations involving international cooperation and alliances, the goods involved are not private. Rather, they exhibit to varying degrees the public traits of jointness of supply and nonexcludability. When a good exhibits jointness, consumption of that good by one person does not diminish the amount available for consumption by another person. If a good is nonexcludable and is provided for one person, it is impossible to prevent another individual from consuming the good, regardless of whether the second individual contributed to the costs of the good's provision or not (Barry and Hardin, 1982:31).[3] Collective defense and a liberal international trading order exhibit these traits of public goods.

With these two traits in mind, and taking Olson's assumptions about personal interactions as valid, it is easy to follow Olson's logic and conclude that a group composed of rational, self-interested individuals will not provide a public good for itself, even though all desire its production. Each individual, when faced with the costs of providing a public good, will opt not to pay his or her share of the provision costs. Recognizing that it is impossible to prevent consumption of the public good once it is produced, each individual sees that it is in his or her best interest not to contribute to the provision of the public good but to take a free ride on the contributions of the other members of the collective. Each in isolation from the others assumes that the others will provide the good, and each thus makes the same decision. Thus the good is not provided.[4] The rational, self-interested decision not to contribute to the provision of the public good results in an inability to increase collective welfare (a result quite similar to the suboptimal, noncooperative equilibrium of the prisoner's dilemma in game theory).

These provision problems arise because, when considering the desired amount of a public good, no individual has an incentive to reveal his or her demand for the good. If, for instance, it is known that the costs of producing the public good will be shared in proportion to each person's demand for the good, no rational person will reveal the personal value he or she places on the production of the good.[5] To the contrary, the individual has every incentive to undervalue his or her demand for the good so as to avoid paying for a portion of public good production. By not paying a full share, but nonetheless maintaining the ability to consume the good, the individual is able to devote more personal resources to the attainment of private goods. In essence, the spillover one individual receives from another individual's production of the public good translates into an increase in the first individual's income, allowing the individual to attain more private goods.

Nevertheless, even though the incentives are such that rational individuals would not contribute to the provision of the public good, there are conditions under which the public good will be provided: (1) if the group is quite small or (2) if one individual, or a small group of individuals, sees an interest in providing the public good without the help of the others in the group (Olson, 1965:2, 49–50). This latter case—the "privileged group" case, in Olson's terminology—prevails when one individual values the production of the good enough that he or she is willing individually to bear the full costs of producing the good. The resulting supply of the public good, however, is not efficiently produced, nor are the costs of production equitably shared. This also leads, by application, to the conventionally accepted analysis of Western security cooperation that suggests that the allies ride free on the defense expenditures of the United States, a characterization of Western alliance cooperation first put forth by Mancur Olson and Richard Zeckhauser (1966).

But this theoretical (and empirical) result becomes suspect when one examines more closely the assumptions upon which Olson based his original work. Olson's "logic," and its subsequent application to alliance affairs by Olson and Zeckhauser, made a number of assumptions that make the model hardly applicable to real-world situations. These assumptions are as follows: (1) Alliance defense is a *pure* public good, that is, fully joint and nonexcludable; (2) alliances produce only a single public good, for example, military defense; (3) alliance security is produced with equal degrees of efficiency in all alliance nations; (4) the costs borne by members of the collective are only economic, meaning that the political costs of alliance membership and security spending are ignored; and (5) allied nations make their decisions about security contributions without consulting the other allies, that is, they exhibit "zero conjectural variations in the sense that each individual regards the behavior of the rest of the community as independent of his own" (Cornes and Sandler, 1984b:367). But while the first of these assumptions has received a great deal of attention in the alliance literature, the remaining assumptions have received less, particularly in terms of empirical analyses of their implications for alliance security cooperation.[6]

Even beyond these unrealistic theoretical assumptions, one is left with a number of nagging intellectual questions raised by the many empirical studies springing from Olson's free-rider hypothesis. First, why should one believe the free-rider hypothesis is valid when it runs counter to the findings of numerous experimental studies of the free-rider problem? These studies (Bohm, 1972; Sweeney, 1973; Scherr and Babb, 1975; Alfano and Marwell, 1981; and Marwell and Ames, 1979, 1980, 1981) have shown under a wide variety of experimental circumstances that the weak free-rider hypothesis (provision of a public good at suboptimal levels) generally does not hold to the extent hypothesized by public goods theory. Even less support was found for the strong free-rider hypothesis (no provision of the public good).

Second—and this directly pertains to the substantive focus of this study—why has the United States apparently been so tolerant of free-riding allies during the post–World War II period? It surely is not due to meekness on the part of the United States, for American policymakers have rarely been at a loss to push the allies in one direction or another, either rhetorically or with the aid of some policy instrument.[7] Except for an occasional member of Congress (like Sam Nunn in the 1980s and Mike Mansfield in 1960s and 1970s), few American policymakers have ever seriously raised the question of military burden sharing beyond the level of political rhetoric.[8] In fact, the Secretary of Defense's *Report on Allied Contributions to the Common Defense* is a generally supportive and upbeat piece documenting allied defense efforts (Cheney, 1990). In other words, although burden sharing is paid a lot of lip service and although it was the original intent of the United States that the allies assume a larger portion of the defense burden, burden sharing has never become a particularly divisive issue.[9]

But if one puts these arguments into the broader security policymaking context discussed earlier, one can begin to find answers to these questions by bringing the strong theoretical assumptions of the Olson and Zeckhauser public goods model closer to real-world approximations. As Susan Strange (1987) argued, the central problem with public goods and game theory approaches to the study of international cooperation is that they assume that international actors are engaged in only one activity at a time, when reality is quite the opposite. More accurately, actors simultaneously participate in a series of bargaining situations at both domestic and international levels and are motivated by changeable goals. Accordingly, this study will show that, because different nations have different political and economic abilities in the pursuit of certain types of policies, nations specialize in their contributions to alliance security in the areas in which they possess political and economic advantages. The efficiency and equity of these specialized contributions in theory, and among Western alliance nations in practice, is the focus of later chapters.

Why Public Goods Theory?

But the question still remains, If there are so many problems with the public goods approach to alliances and international cooperation, why not scrap it and pick up one of a number of other well-developed conceptual and theoretical approaches in the field of international relations? All theories of international cooperation concern themselves in some way with analyzing the ways private and public goods are provided through collective efforts, and so they can shed light on the central focus of public goods theory, even though each approach may do so in an indirect way. For instance, integration theory or functionalism identifies the issue areas where particular goods are provided and goes on to analyze the progression toward political unification. Regime theory focuses on such goods by explaining that norms and procedures are developed among the actors involved to ensure that the goods will be provided. Hegemonic stability theory centers on the enforcement of the arrangements made to provide the goods. And game theory focuses on the incentives for nations to cooperate in the provision of a particular good.

But if one accounts for the limitations of earlier public goods approaches and expands the framework beyond Olson's original boundaries, public goods theory can accomplish all the tasks performed by other theories of cooperation. It also can provide a more comprehensive theoretical approach for the analysis of international cooperation than is provided by the other approaches.

Moreover, in contrast to all the other approaches except possibly game theory in its more complex forms, public goods theory facilitates direct evaluation of the success of the actions taken by members of a

collective in providing the goods in question. Because this study focuses on the pursuit of multidimensional security by nations in the
contemporary international system, the ability to evaluate the contributions made by individual nations in the pursuit of national and
collective security is the goal of this study. The public goods approach
lends itself directly to the evaluation of the inputs and outputs of
security cooperation, in contrast to the other approaches, which are
oriented more to the process of cooperation. I do not discount the
importance of studying the cooperation process but wish to focus this
analysis on the efficiency and equity of the arrangements made by
nations pursuing security collectively.

In essence, public goods theory provides the analyst a rigorous and
systematic theoretical environment. As will be seen in greater detail in
chapter 3, this study does not ignore earlier approaches to international cooperation but rather integrates them into a broad theory of
cooperation. By building upon the rigorous theoretical analysis of
public goods theory and bringing in concepts developed in other
conceptual and theoretical domains, this study provides a richer approach to the problems at hand than is evident in studies that are
based solely on one of the approaches mentioned above. With this
said, the last question for this chapter to answer is, Why study the
Western alliance?

The Past and Future of the Western Alliance System

The future of the Western alliance, and particularly NATO, has been
the subject of much discussion as Eastern bloc countries abandoned
communism and began to liberalize their political and economic systems. Many analysts asked whether NATO could survive when the
threat from the East was eliminated. What happens to a military alliance when the impetus that formed it and that unified it for forty
years is eliminated?

These developments alone provide a powerful rationale for further
study of the relationships that have evolved among the Western nations. Other factors exist, however. First, the Western alliance system
is an excellent example of a cooperative international relationship that
has achieved the goals set out by its founders: deterrence of Soviet
military aggression, economic prosperity, and political stability. In
contrast to other alliances, such as SEATO or METO or ASEAN, the
Warsaw Pact, and even the Andean Group, the Western Alliance
system has unquestionably been a success and should provide insight
into the conditions necessary for the establishment and perpetuation

of international cooperation in an anarchic world. How was the Western alliance able to weather the periodic alliance crises and continue reasonably unaffected since 1949, and what made these countries work to harmonize policies across nations and policy areas?

Second, given the changes that occurred in East-West relations during the late 1980s, I am intrigued by the potential adaptability of the Western alliance system. As the military threat recedes, will the Western alliance system focus on economic and political affairs? With the increasing integration of the European Community, will the cooperation shown among the Group of Seven (G-7) in international monetary affairs continue? Will competition for scarce markets and other trade-related disputes produce cleavages among the North American, European, and Japanese allies as they try to capitalize on the opening markets in the East? Only by understanding the underpinnings of the existing alliance structure can one hope to answer these questions. In essence, one needs to understand the theoretical and conceptual bases for Western cooperation before speculating about the future solidarity and amicability of these relationships.

Finally, studying the Western alliance system has the added advantage of questioning conventional wisdom. Western alliance affairs in all policy realms have quite likely received more American scholarly and popular attention than any other relationship of the post–World War II era. This may have resulted from the historic Atlantic affinities of many Americans or from the centrality of U.S.-Soviet relations in the American mind and electoral system. Whatever the cause, one can hardly look over a list of new publications, examine the new books in a library or bookstore, or open a scholarly international journal without finding some new writing about a facet of the Western alliance. This is not to say that the conventional wisdom is correct: many studies have based their analysis on a model that is far too simplistic to be effectively applied to real-world situations. In other instances, such an integration theory, events have seemingly rendered the hypotheses generated by these theories obsolete, as described by one of the theory's leading proponents (Haas, 1976).

In sum, this study questions many of the ideas found in the conventional wisdom and aims to produce a substantively integrated approach to the analysis of the past and future of the Western alliance that is based on more realistic and more comprehensive theoretical models of international cooperation.

2

Alliance Defense and Collective Action

O LSON AND ZECKHAUSER'S (1966) original model of alliance public goods provision presented an idealized setting for security policymaking. Consistent with this model, the clarifications and expansions of the alliance model made by Bruce Russett (1970), Todd Sandler (1977), and others also proceeded from the assumption that defense policy decisions are made in isolation from other policy considerations. Although some of these later works have suggested that nonmilitary policy considerations are important when making evaluations of defense policy contributions,[1] the implications of these suggestions have never been analyzed in a rigorous theoretical fashion. That task is begun in chapter 3 and the appendixes to the volume and moves us beyond single public good analyses of alliance affairs and into a framework for analysis that assumes policy decisions are made with explicit consideration of decisions in other policy areas.

This chapter lays out the basic theoretical underpinnings of the Olson and Zeckhauser model. The substantive implications of the model, as raised in chapter 1 and developed in later chapters, are peripheral to the discussion at the moment. For the reader unfamiliar with economic theories of alliances, and public goods approaches to international relations more generally, this chapter reviews the earlier material and provides the necessary background for understanding later chapters. For those who are familiar with public goods approaches, this chapter begins the expanded analysis of security cooperation by pointing out where earlier approaches have employed oversimplified assumptions, leaving questions about the empirical findings unanswered. Although other theories of international cooperation (hegemonic stability theory, for example) will not be dissected to the same extent as the Olson and Zeckhauser model, the general questions raised in this chapter—and answered in the next—apply equally well to any theories applied to narrow substantive settings or single-issue areas. I begin with the formal constructs of the simple public goods model.

The Olson and Zeckhauser Approach

Olson and Zeckhauser began their analysis thus: "When a nation decides how large a military force to provide in an alliance, it must consider the value it places on collective defense and the other nondefense goods that must be sacrificed to obtain additional military forces" (1966:268). Growing directly from these remarks, figure 2.1 is a reproduction of the indifference curve map they used (268) to illustrate the effects of opportunity costs on alliance defense provision. The vertical axis in figure 2.1 represents defense expenditure by a given alliance nation. Values above the origin are increasingly negative, and values below it are increasingly positive. Defense capability is measured on the horizontal axis and increases positively from the origin. The indifference curves are labeled U_0 through U_4, with U_0 representing the lowest level of military security of the five curves. The curve $0C$ is the cost curve for the given country.

In isolation from the other alliance countries, a country will obtain $0B$ of defense capability. Point B is the intersection of the horizontal axis and a perpendicular line dropped from point A, the point at which the cost curve $0C$ is tangent to that country's highest indifference curve. But as Olson and Zeckhauser stated, "In an alliance, the amount a nation spends on defense will be affected by the amount its allies provide" (268). This spill-in of defense capability, resulting from the jointness and nonexcludability of the defense public good, can be illustrated by shifting the cost curve in a parallel fashion below the original cost curve so that it intersects the vertical axis at point D (268).[2]

As a result, there is a spill-in of defense expenditures of amount $0D$, symbolizing an increase in income for the nation. Because of this spill-in, the nation receives $0H$ of defense free, and defense capability would seemingly increase from amount $0B$ to amount $0R$. In addition, to obtain this higher defense capability, the nation can spend less on defense than it does in isolation from its allies. More can then be spent on nondefense goods.

The changes in the nation's defense spending in response to different amounts of defense spill-in can be shown by constructing reaction curves. By noting all the points of tangency between the cost curves for various levels of spill-in and the nation's indifference curves, one

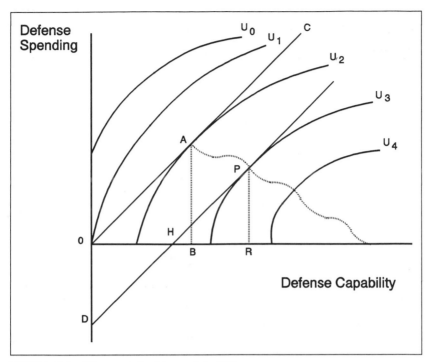

FIGURE 2.1   **Olson and Zeckhauser's indifference map**
Source: Olson and Zeckhauser (1966:268).

can show how these affect production decisions in an alliance nation. As Olson and Zeckhauser put it, "The reaction function indicates how much defense [a] nation will produce for all possible levels of defense expenditure by its allies." Figure 2.2 plots the reaction curves of two alliance nations and corresponds to the figure drawn by Olson and Zeckhauser (268–69).

Figure 2.2 shows that as one nation's defense expenditure increases, the other nation's expenditure tends to decrease: "The intersection point of the two reaction curves indicates how much of the alliance good each ally will supply in equilibrium" (269). Although the curves in this diagram intersect, this need not always be the case. For instance, one nation's reaction curve may totally envelop the other nation's curve, in which case the first nation provides all of the alliance defense and the second nation provides none. The equilibrium supply of defense in this case is thus identical to the isolation supply provided by the first nation (269).

The central problem with the relationships illustrated by figure 2.2, however, is that analyzing alliance defense in this way accounts

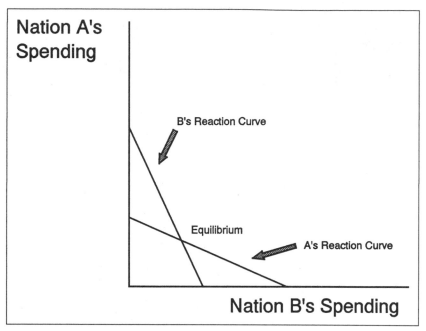

FIGURE 2.2   Olson and Zeckhauser's reaction curves
Source: Olson and Zeckhauser (1966:269, fig. 2).

for only one commodity: military defense. As shown in chapter 3 and later chapters, this is an oversimplification of the policy decisions made by alliance nations. National decisions on defense expenditures are not made in a policy void but rather are subject to trade-offs with other foreign and domestic policy goals. Any budgetary or resource allocation process requires that expenditures in one policy area be balanced with, or at least weighed against, decisions in other policy areas.[3] The recognition that multiple policy tools are considered in the decisionmaking process necessitates, as well, that differences in national productive efficiency must be considered when evaluating alliance security provision. When multiple goods are considered, the distribution of burdens within an alliance may not be the same as suggested throughout this section of the analysis. Nonetheless, the discussion proceeds under these simplified assumptions.

The defense expenditure decisions made by alliance nations "are such that the 'larger' nation—the one that places the higher absolute value on the alliance good—will bear a disproportionately large share of the common burden" (269). This concept of absolute value becomes clearer when one extends Olson and Zeckhauser's analysis to a present-day example. Because of the geographic and economic size and the

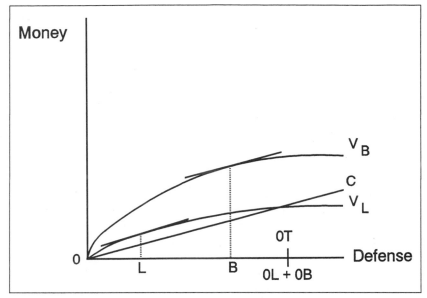

FIGURE 2.3   Olson and Zeckhauser's evaluation curves
Source: Olson and Zeckhauser (1966:269).

global role of the United States, it necessarily has greater military defense requirements than do other NATO nations. The Netherlands, for instance—because of the small geographic region it must defend and the scope of its international commitments—would not have chosen to spend $281 billion on its military force.[4] Using the Olson and Zeckhauser model, one would hypothesize that the Netherlands would be a free rider on the American defense effort.

Figure 2.3 presents this argument graphically, showing evaluation curves for two alliance nations, called Big Atlantis and Little Atlantis by Olson and Zeckhauser. The curves show that Big Atlantis places a higher absolute value on defense, as indicated by the steeper slope of curve V_B, than does Little Atlantis. In addition, this diagram assumes that both nations maximize their utility with reference to the same cost curve, $0C$.

However, this model's assumptions pull the analysis away from practical applications. The central problem with the multinational application of the cost curve is that costs of production for any good are rarely the same across national economies. Olson and Zeckhauser gloss over the potential positive effects of consideration of cost variations and comparative advantages in production. (The implications of this simplification are a focus of chapter 3 and the appendixes and yield substantial differences in the interpretations of alliance security burden sharing than those put forth in this chapter.)

Nevertheless, in Olson and Zeckhauser's model, both countries in isolation would produce defense to the point where the slope of their evaluation curves equaled the slope of the cost curve—in other words, at the point where marginal value equals marginal cost. The amounts of defense produced by Big and Little Atlantis are, in this case, 0*B* and 0*L,* respectively. But once an alliance forms, if the two national production levels hold constant, the two nations will be consuming 0*B plus* 0*L* of defense, or amount 0*T* in figure 2.3. At that level of consumption, marginal value is less than marginal cost, and the two nations will reduce their aggregate defense production accordingly to arrive at an equilibrium level of alliance defense production, in which marginal value and cost are equal. This is the point at which Big Atlantis produces 0*B* of defense and Little Atlantis produces no defense at all (269–70). Alliance defense burdens are disproportionate, with Little Atlantis as the consummate free rider.

The crux of the problem, in terms of both optimality and equity of public good provision, is the conflict between the conditions for individual utility maximization and those for optimality of public good provision. An individual will produce at the point where marginal cost (*MC*) equals the marginal rate of substitution of money for the public good (*MRS*). In equilibrium, then, the marginal rate of substitution of Country 1 will equal the marginal rate of substitution of Country 2, which will equal the marginal cost of production. That is

$$MRS_1 = MRS_2 = \ldots MRS_n = MC.$$

But for an optimal quantity of a public good to be produced, the sum of the marginal rates of substitution of each alliance nation must equal marginal cost (ibid., 269–71).

$$MRS_1 + MRS_2 + \ldots MRS_n = MC.$$

In equilibrium, Big Atlantis's *MRS* equals its marginal cost. Little Atlantis produces nothing, and its *MRS* exceeds marginal cost and is rather large.[5] Mathematically, in equilibrium or also when producing at isolation levels, the sum of both countries' marginal rates of substitution exceeds marginal costs. To rectify that result and to reach optimal defense provision, one or both nations would need to move outward on their evaluation curves to points where the slopes of the curves become gentle enough that the sum of the two *MRS*'s equals the marginal cost of defense production; that is, the sum equals the slope of alliancewide cost curve *C.* Moreover, for defense burdens to be proportionate to size, the marginal cost of defense production must be shared proportionately: if one nation is twice the size of another, the first nation must produce twice the amount of alliance defense as the second (270). There is, however, no individually rational reason for increased production or marginal cost sharing, and optimal provision of the public good will not occur.

One runs into additional problems with this conception of alliance affairs when one considers that, in the independent adjustment process, alliance nations make their security policy decisions without consulting each other. But such an assumption is unrealistic in alliances that form to protect common security interests. To assume that alliance nations make their military expenditure decisions without some consultation with their allies is overly restrictive. In the Western alliance, intra-alliance consultation and official interaction take place informally at NATO headquarters in Brussels and, more formally, at annual ministerial meetings, periodic NATO summits, Group of Seven (G-7) meetings, and Western economic summits, to name only a few of the forums for interaction. Granted, actual expenditures are decided upon domestically, but general goals are collective decisions. The 1978 decision to increase spending by 3 percent above inflation is one such instance; the G-5 and G-7 meetings in 1985 and 1987, respectively, regarding the American international economic imbalances and the value of the dollar are others. At a theoretical level, the introduction of consultation to the alliance model has significant effects on the optimality of alliance security provision.

In addition to their theoretical model, Olson and Zeckhauser's article tested the model empirically with data on fourteen NATO countries for the years 1960 and 1964. Correlating gross national product (GNP) with defense expenditures as a percentage of the 1964 GNP, they found "a significant positive correlation indicating that the large nations in NATO bear a disproportionate share of the burden of the common defense" (275). Further evidence of suboptimality and the lack of marginal cost sharing was seen when Olson and Zeckhauser correlated GNP with the quotient of each national defense budget divided by the percentage of total NATO infrastructure costs borne by each nation for 1960. They found a significant positive correlation, validating the hypothesis that burdens are shared more equitably on alliance expenditures when marginal cost sharing is explicitly fostered than when it is not. Examining infrastructure costs alone, they found a significant negative correlation between national income and the percentage of national income devoted to infrastructure costs, which further validated their model's hypotheses (276–77).[6]

Evidently, Olson and Zeckhauser's economic theory of alliances presents a verifiable model of alliance behavior that fits with the empirical evidence. Their results, moreover, have been supported by the findings of Oneal and Elrod (1989) and Oneal (1990a, 1990b). Yet the model used in—and empirically supported by—these studies leaves a number of theoretical questions unanswered. First, is it appropriate to use a model that assumes that alliance goods are pure public goods? If not, what difference does it make in the analysis, theoretically and empirically? Second, when we relax our assumptions that national costs of production are identical and consider the provision of multiple goods by an alliance, what effect does this have on the Olson and Zeckhauser results? The assumption that alliance decisions on defense expenditures are made without consideration of other policy decisions is needlessly strong. Third, can the effects of consultation among alliance members be disregarded in any model of alliance security provision? This seems unlikely when we consider the persuasion the United States has used since World War II to obtain agreements from its allies.

Refinements of the Single Public Goods Model: The Work of Russett, Sandler, and Others

Bruce Russett, in his book *What Price Vigilance?* (1970), found that, although the United States ranked at the top of NATO military expenditures, the strength of the correlation between military spending and the gross national product found by Olson and Zeckhauser declined from about 1961 onward. He also found that, aside from a few deviant cases such as Portugal in the early 1960s, "all nations (except Iceland) [made] some military expenditures for their apparent 'private' benefits" (109–10). His work questioned whether the "pure" public goods model was an accurate appraisal of NATO burden sharing over time.

But where Russett began by identifying some empirical incongruity in the Olson and Zeckhauser model, Todd Sandler and his associates (Sandler and Cauley, 1975; Sandler, 1977; Sandler and Forbes, 1980; Sandler, Cauley, and Forbes, 1980; Murdoch and Sandler, 1982, 1984) built on Russett's work, refining the model by focusing on variations in the purity of alliance defense and the implications of these impurities for efficiency and equity in the provision of the alliance good. Drawing on Mark Pauly's (1970) classification scheme for evaluating the ways in which a good exhibits "publicness," Sandler and his associates focused on the existence of military defense goods that are (1) public within a country but private between countries (Pauly's Case 3) or (2) impurely public both within and between countries (a variation on Pauly's Case 2). Under Sandler's "joint product model," the Olson and Zeckhauser model and its empirical results are a special case in a more general theory of military alliances that encompasses all types of alliance military goods (Sandler and Cauley, 1975:333–35). Olson and Zeckhauser dealt only with pure public goods. Nonetheless, Sandler and his associates continued to employ other simplifying assumptions used by Olson and Zeckhauser: (1) that single public good analyses are the relevant level of analysis, (2) that production costs are constant across nations, and (3) that allies make their production decisions without consulting other alliance members and without coordinating their policies with other allies.[7]

Sandler and Forbes argued that alliance military expenditures produce some goods that are public within a nation but private between alliance nations (1980:429). In other words, some military goods produced under the auspices of alliance defense produce private benefits for the producing nation. In contrast to the alliancewide consumption of public goods, these joint products have two portions available for consumption: one portion is consumed by the nation, while another portion is available for consumption by the entire alliance. For example, a soldier's weapon that is used both for maintenance of domestic order and as an infantry weapon for the alliance is a joint product. The development of an arms industry as a spin-off of alliance defense is also a joint product. Because of the private benefits obtained through joint products, national allocations to alliance military efforts tend to be somewhat higher than they would be in the pure public goods case (429).

As for Sandler's second type of impurity, an understanding of the concept of congestion in public goods consumption is useful. With pure public goods, the assumption is made that one unit of public goods produced by Country A results in a consumable externality of one unit of goods for Country B. But as Buchanan (1968) and others (e.g., Oakland, 1969, 1972; Head and Shoup, 1969, 1973) have shown, a continuum of goods exists from purely public to purely private. Many goods considered public goods actually yield less than one unit of externality per unit produced, thus not resting at the public pole of the goods continuum. Lower externality levels result because most public goods become congested as greater numbers of individuals consume them. For example, parks are public goods for surrounding neighborhoods, and residents can consume the parks with relatively little diminution of their facilities. But as the population grows and parks are used more heavily, the public goods begin to show signs of congestion: grass wears thin, swings break, and there are not enough basketball courts. The parks no longer provide the same benefits to each individual.[8]

Sandler argued that congestion can and does occur in the provision of alliance defense. He used the term *thinning* to describe what happens to military forces that exhibit rivalry in their consumption (Sandler, 1977:449). This concept is of special relevance in studies that focus on "conventional war alliances" (448), for conventional weapons and the public goods they engender for the alliance exhibit higher congestion than do nuclear weapons. Because conventional weapons can serve purposes other than military defense, such as keeping domestic order and "providing national relief in times of disaster" (444), they may be consumed to a higher degree by the nation deploying them than by other nations. The spatial limits of military forces and considerations of force mobility also lead to congestion of alliance defense goods. Thus the nature of the weaponry has a significant impact upon the purity of the public goods and also influences the provision of these goods. Olson and Zeckhauser hinted at these impurities in their original work (1966:272–73) but did not develop their implications.

The continuum of weaponry allows us to judge the nature of an alliance's military production. Conceptually, this continuum involves the traditional distinction made in national security studies between deterrence and defense (see Snyder, 1961). As Sandler put it:

> The distinction between deterrence and protection [defense] is dependent upon such factors as action versus threat, credibility, information flows and the ultimate capabilities of the weapons. Deterrence requires the threat of retaliation and is closely tied to an information flow relaying threats and counterthreats between alliances. . . . In contrast, protection primarily relies on action rather than threat. Since protective action concerns a fending off of an assault, protection achieves this goal by relying on secrecy. (1977:445)

This is a rather fuzzy distinction, but considering the characteristics of various modern weapons, it is significant. For instance, during the 1950s, American defense policy, as represented by the statements of John Foster Dulles and others, centered upon the doctrine of massive retaliation. This doctrine stated that American and allied military security against Soviet aggression rested on the threat of nuclear retaliation. American conventional forces were demobilized, and only a small capability existed to repel a Soviet attack without resort to nuclear weapons. In many respects, the Eisenhower administration's effort to provide low-cost security forced the Western allies to rely primarily on this preventive posture rather than develop a mix of conventional and nuclear options. Most important, reliance on massive nuclear retaliation allowed the Western allies to depend on the United States for their military security because of the American monopoly on nuclear weapons.

With the adoption of flexible response in the late 1960s and its implementation in the early 1970s, Western military security shifted away from a deterrent posture to one in which protective weapons would provide an active defense. Sandler and his colleagues (Sandler and Forbes, 1980; Murdoch and Sandler, 1982, 1984) have shown that this shift in NATO's posture had a significant impact on the distribution of burdens among the allies, because of the larger private benefits accruing to individual alliance goods providers than is the case with deterrent goods.

In Sandler's continuum of alliance military forces (1977:448), at one pole lies a military force that relies totally on deterrent weapons, a force that might be possessed by a nation deploying only nuclear weapons, assuming that the weapons were deployed only for retaliatory purposes and not for warfighting. This force would have little utility as protection against an actual attack. At the other pole lies a military force composed of only protective weapons, including air defense systems, antiballistic missile systems, and civil defense programs (445). This military force would have little deterrent or retaliatory value other than increasing the aggressor's uncertainty of success. Deterrent weapons yield nearly pure public goods and therefore show little congestion, while protective weapons produce almost no public externality and are highly congestive.

When an alliance adopts a particular military posture and deploys the weapons that accompany it, these choices, according to Sandler, have a direct influence upon the types of goods produced by the alliance and on the optimality of the output. If an alliance takes the form of a nuclear war alliance and relies primarily on nuclear deterrence and minimal conventional capabilities for its security (as did NATO in the 1950s and early 1960s), it is located near the purely deterrent end of the continuum, and the goods produced are largely public goods with minor congestion costs (448). If the United States intended to guarantee peace and security through nuclear deterrence, it would produce goods that are joint and nonexcludable. The extension of the American nuclear umbrella to one more nation would result in little or no decrease in the credibility of the guarantee (low congestion costs) because of the characteristics and global deployments of American nuclear weapons systems. The umbrella is nonexcludable, in most instances, because of the global effects of nuclear warfare.[9] If one nation can consume the goods of prevention of nuclear holocaust, so can others. In addition, the geography of the American nuclear guarantee results in large degrees of excludability: for instance, once the guarantee was extended to Italy, Belgium and the Netherlands were able to consume this public good without paying for its provision.

According to Sandler's analysis, then, nuclear war alliances should exhibit a rather high level of free riding and produce suboptimal levels of the alliance good.[10]

A conventional war alliance is located closer than a nuclear war alliance to the protective weapons pole of the continuum and produces a higher level of private goods (448). Alliances of this type produce military goods that yield a variety of benefits, some purely public, some purely private, some in between these extremes (Sandler and Forbes, 1980:426). When such a variety of goods is produced by individual national expenditures on alliance defense, the tendency toward suboptimality is decreased. As the percentage of private benefits as a portion of total alliance benefits rises (resulting from an increasingly large proportion of protective weapons in the alliance arsenal), individual nations have a greater incentive to contribute to the provision of alliance military goods. Because these goods exhibit high rivalries of consumption, a nation in this type of alliance must spend more on defense to achieve a given level of security than if the goods were more public and the nation could consume the production of other nations. As a result, conventional war alliances would produce closer to optimal levels of alliance goods than is the case in the Olson and Zeckhauser model.

Sandler further asserted that, while the Olson and Zeckhauser model provides a useful theoretical construct for the study of alliances, it should be viewed as a special case in a more general theory, as illustrated by the continuum of alliance types conceptualized in the joint product model (Sandler and Cauley, 1975). Sandler and his associates maintained that Olson and Zeckhauser's model applies only to nuclear war alliances, in which alliance military goods are largely pure public goods. The model provides a very loose fit for the activities of conventional war alliances, which yield much higher levels of private goods. The joint product model, by contrast, creates a framework for evaluating the types of goods produced by alliances.

But problems arise with Sandler's framework when one tries to fit weapon systems into deterrent or defense classifications. The suggestion that nuclear weapons are deterrent weapons and that conventional weapons are protective weapons is too restrictive when dealing with the characteristics of many modern weapons systems. Nuclear warfighting strategies, especially at the tactical level, could be classified as protective because of their declared intent to be a rung on the ladder of escalation from conventional forces to nuclear forces.[11] Nuclear weapons programs, moreover, yield many private benefits, such as research and development funding and civilian economy spin-offs. Modern conventional weapons with high accuracy and large explosive yields fit as closely with deterrent strategies as they do with defense. It is difficult to separate the private and public benefits that different types of weaponry provide, much less classify each system as deterrent or defensive. As a result, testing the joint product model in a direct way is fraught with conceptual ambiguity.

Nonetheless, the indirect empirical testing of the joint-product model performed by Sandler and his associates tends to support the general hypothesis

> that as an alliance moves toward the protective pole, there will be less of a systematic relationship between the size of GDP and "defense effort." An ally's "defense effort" should be unrelated to its size, since an increase in the incidence of private and/or excludable public benefits should stimulate preference revelation and generate, as well as maintain, an increase in "defense effort" irrespective of industrial size. (Sandler and Forbes, 1980:436)

The empirical tests Sandler used have been at only the aggregate defense spending level. No attempts were made to disaggregate alliance military expenditures using his classification system to test how certain weapon expenditure categories fit with the specific hypotheses of the joint product model. This is the logical way to test Sandler's weapons classification system, but one would ultimately run into classification problems.

At the aggregate level, nonetheless, the results of rank-order correlations performed on data for the NATO countries show that, for the years 1960–66, the predictions of the Olson and Zeckhauser model held. After this time period, the strength of the correlations between the GDP and the ratio of military expenditure to GDP declined, supporting the prediction of the joint product model regarding NATO's adoption of flexible response in the late 1960s and the subsequent increase in the production of private goods by the alliance (436–38).

In an effort to capture the benefits received by individual NATO members, Sandler and Forbes developed a composite measure of benefits gained by an individual NATO nation. This was done by first computing the percentage of the whole of NATO accounted for by a single nation's three variables (population, GDP, and exposed border) and then taking the arithmetic mean of those three percentages. For instance, in 1960 Canada accounted for 3.76 percent of NATO's population, 4.39 percent of its GDP, and 20.02 percent of its exposed border, averaging 9.39 percent of total NATO benefits received. This figure was compared with the nation's total defense burden. Canada's 1960 defense burden was 2.64 percent of the NATO total. This figure supports the notion that Canada was free riding on other nations' defense efforts in that year, because of the large discrepancy between burden and benefits (439).

As the joint product model hypothesizes, comparing benefits received to burdens borne by NATO nations for the years 1960 and 1975 shows that, while the United States overcontributed to alliance defense, about 6 percent of the alliance's military burden shifted onto the European allies during that period. Italy and Canada remained the two largest free riders, while others who provided deterrent weapons to the alliance (France, the United Kingdom, and the United States) or received large amounts of private benefits from alliance defense (West Germany) approached—or in the case of the United States, exceeded—their fair share of contribution (439–40).

Using multivariate regression techniques, Murdoch and Sandler (1982, 1984) found further empirical support for the hypotheses of the joint product model. They found support for Olson and Zeckhauser's GDP-military expenditure correlation (1982, 259), but as before, they also found that this positive correlation decreased with NATO's implementation of flexible response. Interestingly enough, at least two of the larger NATO nations—West Germany and the United Kingdom—continued to free ride on other nations' defense efforts. Canada and Turkey also were free riders (261). The basic results of this analysis are supported by Murdoch and Sandler (1984), who found that the income elasticity of demand for military expenditures increased over the 1961–79 period (96). Flexible response has helped redistribute the defense burden among the allies and has decreased suboptimality in alliance defense provision. This distinction between flexible response and nuclear weapons spending is supported by the findings of Hansen, Murdoch, and Sandler (1990).

In each study, Canada was found undercontributing to alliance defense; in Sandler and Forbes (1980), Italy and Canada are shown as free riders, and West Germany and the United Kingdom continued free riding even under flexible response (Murdoch and Sandler, 1982). In their study of the differential impact of conventional versus nuclear spending, Hansen, Murdoch, and Sandler (1990) found that West Germany and France, among other allies, reduced their conventional spending "in response to an increase in strategic [nuclear] spending." This shows that five of the larger NATO members free ride on the military efforts of other Western nations.

Findings like these for large alliance nations are anomalies in the original public goods model of alliances. But these findings are not the only ones that point to fundamental problems with this thesis. In Sandler's studies and many others (e.g., Oneal and Elrod, 1989; Oneal, 1990a, 1990b; Oneal and Diehl, 1990; Boyer, 1989, 1990), heavy military burdens relative to GDP were borne by small countries like Greece, Turkey, and Portugal. Granted, each had nonalliance concerns that required large defense expenditures, but these forces continued to be placed under NATO's integrated command and, therefore, contradict the simple public goods model.

Conclusion

The model of alliance security provision presented in this chapter provides strong evidence of free riding in allied defense expenditures. Not only has this model been given great credence in the academic realm, but it is at the root of the persistent accusations of free riding that the United States makes about its allies. Although it is rarely part of the official foreign policy stance of the president or the Pentagon, the thought that America's allies do not do enough for the common defense is often implicit in policy statements and frequently explicit in congressional speeches. From a domestic political standpoint, ally bashing is a popular pastime, particularly when allocations to overseas commitments mean cuts in domestic programs. It is not difficult to see how influential this model has been in American policy toward its allies.

Nevertheless, to say that a model is popularly accepted is not the same as saying that the model is accurate. It simply indicates that the model has provided a simple and popularly accessible way to characterize alliance relations. But alliance politics are far from simple, and many decisions are beyond the understanding of the average citizen. So the reader—and particularly the scholar—who tries to decipher the theory and practice of alliance affairs must be wary of models of reality whose assumptions pull us far from the complexity of international affairs.

The original public goods model has done this. It makes the following restrictive assumptions. (1) Alliance defense is a pure public good, (2) alliances produce only a single public good, (3) the alliance public good is produced with equal degrees of efficiency in all alliance nations, (4) the costs borne by allies are only economic or monetary, and (5) allied nations make their security decisions without consulting other allies. Sandler and his associates have dealt quite effectively with the implications of the first of these assumptions, but the others remain divorced from the practical constructs of international relations. Accordingly, we will reexamine the findings of the original alliance model more closely.

3

Why Nations Cooperate

THE POPULAR IMAGE of Western alliance affairs holds that since 1945 the United States has borne an inordinate military burden for allies that do little to provide for their own defense, even though these allies are capable of providing for their own defense. In the political realm, this image leads to ally bashing by members of Congress and is politically exploited at election time. In the scholarly realm, this image (and supporting data) is used to validate the free-rider hypothesis of Paul Samuelson (1954), Mancur Olson (1965), and others. Even accounting for the private benefits of military spending received by individual alliance members (e.g., maintaining internal stability and defense spin-offs to civilian consumption), there is support for the hypothesis of the free-loading ally.

But the consistency and actual robustness of these free-rider results remain in question. Most of the literature on Western alliance security policies frequently refer to nonmilitary policies both in public statements by decisionmakers and in scholarly studies. As a result, an analysis of security cooperation in contemporary international affairs must look beyond military expenditures. The single public good model of alliance defense (and free riding), first put forth by Olson and Zeckhauser, must be expanded to account for the provision of multiple public and private goods within the alliance setting.

In this chapter I examine the validity of the underlying assumptions of that model and move those assumptions closer to real-world approximations. I start by presenting the theory of comparative advantage as developed in the international trade literature as a way of critically examining the simple model's assumptions that (1) alliances produce only a single public good, namely, military defense, and (2) alliance defense is produced with equal efficiency in all alliance nations (i.e., each nation is confronted with a cost curve identical to that of its allies). Next, I examine the assumption that the costs of alliance contributions as calculated by national decisionmakers are purely economic. In other words, I question the fact that little account is generally taken of the political costs associated with alliance membership and contributions. Last, I discuss the implications of the assumption that allied nations make their security contribution decisions without consulting the other allies—that allies exhibit "zero conjectural variations in the sense that each individual regards the behavior of the rest of the community as independent of his own" (Cornes and Sandler, 1984b:367). By examining the four restrictive assumptions of the simple public goods model (see chap. 2), I move toward a richer theory of alliance and international cooperation. The new theoretical framework also yields a more optimistic appraisal of the prospects for international cooperation and more efficient and equitable collective outcomes in the contemporary international system.

The following is also the theoretical groundwork for the analysis of multi-issue security cooperation in the Western alliance that comes in later chapters. Two appendixes (see end of book) present alternative formal models of alliance public good provision. These models provide the foundation for the theoretical critique that follows. The appendix models played an instrumental role in my thinking on the material, and I encourage readers to examine them.

An Intersection of Theory and Policy

Stanley Sloan (1985a) pointed to some differences in the ways the allies approach Western security concerns in the Third World. He identified a European tendency to devote larger resources than the United States to political and economic security in the Third World. Aside from France, and to a lesser extent the United Kingdom, the European allies have limited military projection capabilities outside the immediate NATO region and, therefore, must rely on nonmilitary tools in out-of-area activities. The common historical, cultural, and linguistic ties between the Europeans and the Third World also facilitate the use of these tools (35–37). These affinities provide political sources of comparative advantage in the production of alliance security goods. In support of his assertions, Sloan cited the following passage from the 1980 British white paper on defense:

> The best answer [to Western security problems in the Third World] is to try to remove the sources of regional instability which create opportunities for outside intervention. In some circumstances, military resources will not be appropriate at all; in others they may form only one component of the total response. Diplomacy, development aid and trade policies will usually have a greater contribution to make. (37)

A similar sentiment was expressed by Harold Brown, secretary of defense under President Carter: "It would be a mistake to concentrate all of our attention [and] the bulk of our resources on the arms race. The competition [with the U.S.S.R.] reaches into other areas as well, and we have comparative advantages in them" (Brown, 1982:10).

Naturally, then, one can hypothesize that some allies will devote relatively greater resources to political and economic assistance than others even though all aim toward the maintenance of alliance security objectives. In any case, development aid given by Western alliance nations to Third World countries provides not only private benefits to the aid donor but also public benefits to the whole alliance, by promoting pro-Western sentiments, political stability, and commercial stability. Additionally, because of negative sentiment toward American hegemony in the world, the United States may receive more purely public spillover from allied aid donations than the allies receive from American donations.

In another policy realm, Henning Wegener, NATO's assistant secretary general for political affairs, has written that the alliance is committed to enlivening "its traditional co-operation in the scientific realm and on environmental matters with new initiatives," emphasizing the value of NATO's "third dimension" (1989:7). The final declaration from the June 1989 summit put it succinctly: "Convinced of the vital need for international cooperation in science and technology, and its beneficial effect on global security, we have for several decades maintained Alliance programmes of scientific cooperation" (U.S. Department of State, 1989:4). Research and development cooperation, as implied in these passages, produces significant public results by increasing the knowledge base accessible to all nations. In addition, particularly for those findings with military application, such spending by alliance nations has implications for Western military defense efforts. Participation in the activities of the Coordinating Committee (COCOM) for multilateral export controls, although not directly related to research and development spending, can also produce a public good for Western countries by limiting technology transfer to adversary economies.[1]

When these ideas are placed in the context of the following assertion, the breadth and depth of Western alliance cooperation can be fully appreciated: the Western alliance, according to Wallace Theis (1989:358), was founded as (and continues to be) a "permanent and integrated" organization, whose members "pool their resources and establish the organizational machinery for nearly continuous consultations on the direction the collective efforts should take." While national autonomy is the rule for Western alliance nations, a degree of security policy integration can be identified during the postwar era. Forums for such interaction exist informally at NATO headquarters in Brussels and, more formally, at the regular ministerial meetings, the periodic NATO summits, Group of Seven negotiations, and Western summits. Given the overlap of these various forums, none of these organizations is a discrete entity where only narrow policy concerns are discussed. Instead, each forum addresses similar issues and concerns from its own unique direction. In that way, each forum is charged with helping to manage some aspect of Western security policies.

Allied cooperation during the 1990–91 Persian Gulf crisis is a case in point. Initial consultations in the NATO Council addressed desired military responses, while economic forums such as the Group of Seven planned for the management of the macroeconomic ramifications of the crisis and war, for example, the threats to economic stability as a result of fluctuations in oil prices. With the changing nature of the Soviet threat, NATO reassessed its need for nuclear first use and significant forward deployment, while the nations in the G-7 and Western economic summits debated the need for (and types of) Western economic aid to Eastern Europe and the Soviet Union.

Thus expenditure categories other than military are considered important by the allies and, therefore, should be included in any evaluation of Western alliance burden sharing. This does not imply that the several examples of additional expenditure categories mentioned here are the only ones appropriate for analysis; on the contrary, numerous other policy tools (e.g., Western cooperation to maintain international monetary and economic stability, Third World debt refinancing, and political solidarity within the alliance) should be examined, although some are beyond the scope of this study. The interaction of these policy tools in the alliance security setting is the subject of the following theoretical expansion of the original single public goods model.

The Logic of Public Goods Trade

Countries trade with each other because different prices exist for the same goods. If every nation could produce every good it desired at the same price as every other nation, there would be no reason to trade. But because every nation is endowed with different amounts and qualities of the various factors of production—land, labor, and capital, to name only three—one nation will produce some goods more cheaply than other countries. When economies open to one another and they recognize these price differentials, common interests are identified, and trade begins. To use David Ricardo's example, if Britain can produce cloth relatively cheaper than Portugal, and Portugal can produce wine relatively cheaper than Britain, Britain will specialize in the production of cloth and sell it to Portugal, and Portugal will produce wine and sell it to Britain.

I use the word *relatively* to indicate that absolute differences in price need not exist for trade to benefit all countries. Rather, an individual country need only have a relative, or comparative, advantage in the production of a particular good to gain from specialization and trade. Even if one country can produce every good more efficiently (and thus sell every good more cheaply) than other countries, the other countries can still gain from trading with the efficient producer by producing the goods for which they are relatively more efficient. Even if Portugal can produce both wine and cloth more cheaply than Britain, Britain can still sell cloth to Portugal, if Britain is more efficient in cloth production than in wine production as measured by Portugal's costs of cloth and wine production. Thus, in almost every conceivable real-world situation, possibilities for beneficial trade exist, because only comparative advantages, not absolute ones, need be recognized and exploited by the trading countries.

But problems arise with notions of comparative advantage and trade when public rather private goods are considered. In the single public goods model laid out in chapter 2, no incentive exists for a smaller alliance nation to trade for the public good of military defense if a larger nation is already providing that good. In that simple model, there is no incentive for trade, because the model ignores the multiple goods produced by the alliance and also ignores the degree that allies consult with one another on security policies. When constructing a model with the more realistic assumptions outlined above, the incentives for trade in public goods follow a logic similar to that of Ricardo's theory of comparative advantage. Additionally, not only is the logic of specialization and trade similar, but trade in public goods also yields benefits for the trading nations similar to those obtained through trade in private goods. Trade in public goods increases efficiency and security in the alliance setting.

A number of studies, beginning with two by Olson and Zeckhauser (1967, 1970), have reconsidered the implications of the identical cross-national costs assumption and have pointed to more optimistic scenarios for public goods provision. In their two follow-up studies, Olson and Zeckhauser suggested that increased alliance defense provision could be achieved if alliance members specialized in the production of military goods in line with their individual comparative advantages: "The relatively most efficient producers of a given external economy should 'specialize' in that externality, and receive different spillovers or ordinary goods in return" (1970:516). Their argument, however, continued to view alliance security provision as a military question alone, and thus specialization was concerned only with military production. A similar substantive critique can be made of a study by Philip Jones (1988) that arrived at parallel conclusions about the positive welfare effects of intra-alliance trade (139).

The trading case for public goods has been presented more formally in several other works (Connolly, 1970, 1972; Loehr, 1973; and Kiesling, 1974). Herbert Kiesling showed that, by introducing differences in productive efficiency and rational consultation between countries, moves toward Pareto optimality are possible.[2] By constructing public goods offer curves for this trading case, Kiesling showed that, although moves toward an optimal solution were possible, the actual public goods provision outcome is still likely to be suboptimal.[3] The exact outcome will exhibit specialization in production along comparative advantage lines and be determined by the relative bargaining abilities and the power of the individuals involved. Nevertheless, in this model of public goods trade, if any trade at all occurs (trade is the rational choice in Kiesling's model because of the introduction of consultation), the public good will be provided more efficiently than if no trade occurred, as in the Nash provision process. Appendix B presents a revised version of Kiesling's model.

In another study, Albert Breton (1970:884) addressed the possibilities for the provision of multiple public goods by assuming that "bargaining, exchange and negotiation" do take place among members of a collective, even though they may not be "conducted in a smooth and easy way." Directly relating to the two assumptions at hand, he argued that "restricting the number of alternatives in negotiation to one would increase the chances of negotiation failing, especially if the distribution of preferences was of a special kind. On the other hand, increasing the number of alternatives does increase the chances for cooperation" (901). The heart of Breton's argument rests on the notion that, as more goods become relevant to the collective, there will be greater possibilities that spillovers can be exchanged because of variations in the intensity of preferences held by the members of the collective (900).

When involved in negotiations on the provision of multiple goods, each ally will give in on points where preferences are weak and stand firm where they are strong. As the number of goods increases, every member of the collective will be likely to win an individually important battle or two in the negotiating process. In the alliance security case, this can mean that the alliance will adopt some policies that fit with an individual country's preferred mix of security policy tools, and at other times this same country may disagree with alliance choices but will not object in order to maintain alliance solidarity and because of potential future wins.[4] Differences in policy preferences can be beneficial to alliance security interests in that they may lead some allies to tolerate free riding in a particular policy area as long as the apparent free riders are doing their part in other areas. Trade in public goods among alliance members increases the efficiency of alliance security provision—and alliance security itself—even if individual allies do not obtain their ideal policy choices or exact preferences (see appendixes).

The possibilities for public goods trade, especially as characterized by Breton, are corroborated outside the narrow public goods approach by ideas generated by game theory and other rational choice approaches to international relations. In particular, the study of issue linkage yields some interesting insights into the effects of linkage on the possibilities for obtaining international agreements and the potential that such agreements can move collective outcomes toward Pareto optimality.

In one study of linkage, Robert Tollison and Thomas Willett pointed to international issue linkage as a way to promote cooperation when explicit side payments on a single issue are not possible and agreement on that issue is blocked (1979:437).[5] But if two issues can be linked that provide benefits on one issue to the first country and benefits on the other issue to the second country (quite similar to Breton's reasoning), then agreement could be secured on both issues even though agreement on either issue individually is in doubt. Robert Keohane (1984) argued similarly when explaining that the clustering of issues under an international regime makes "more potential *quids* . . . available for the *quo*" (90). Such conclusions about the value of linkage are echoed by Michael McGinnis (1986), James Sebenius (1983, 1984), Bernard Hoekman (1989), William Wallace (1976), Kenneth Oye (1979), and Howard Raiffa (1982). By dealing with multiple issues simultaneously, alliance nations can discover which nations have productive advantages and are thus able to put these advantages to the best individual and collective use.

Issue linkage, or the relevance of multiple public goods, does not simply facilitate agreement among rational international actors. More important—fitting with the hypotheses of Olson and Zeckhauser, Connolly, Jones and Kiesling—studies of issue linkage and multiple games have concluded that linking issues will also push agreements closer to the Pareto frontier. Tollison and Willett (1976:98) asserted that aggregating issues allows agreements to be made that lie closer to the contract curve (the locus of optimal agreements) than is possible if the agreements are arrived at individually.

In a study of "games in multiple arenas," or nested games, George Tsebelis (1990) pushed this point even farther, stating that decisions made in one arena may actually appear suboptimal or irrational to someone examining only the single-issue area. But when the decisions and their outcomes are placed inside a more complicated, multiple-issue setting, decisionmakers may view these decisions as optimizing and efficient (9). Tsebelis went even farther along this line of theoretical development by noting that the introduction of communication and bargaining to the multiple-issue setting can produce the same cooperative result for a single-play game, as has been identified by Axelrod, Keohane, and others for single-issue, iterative games (183).

Arthur Stein (1980) added that successful issue linkage also requires that the nations involved in the agreement be interdependent—that decisions made by one nation effect the problems, choices, and decisions faced by the other party (79–80). More to the point of the present critique, greater interdependence among the actors involved in security cooperation will provide more issues to link and, therefore, moves back to Breton's argument and Keohane's *quids* and *quo*. This has direct relevance to the substantive material of this study, considering the interdependence among the Western alliance countries. In the end, considerations of multiple goods not only facilitates agreements but promotes specialization and moves the collective outcome closer to an optimal solution. All these ideas fall in line with the theoretical constructs of international trade theory.

The Introduction of Political Comparative Advantage

Rational choice approaches to the study of international cooperation provide a powerful tool for analysis. Their strength lies in the way economic rationality is used to model decisionmaking. The assumption of economic rationality can be mistakenly extended, however, and be confused with considerations of the costs borne by members of a collective. The costs borne by the actors under examination are often confined to economic profit or loss. Certainly, the use of percentage of gross national product spent on the military as the standard measure of burden sharing in alliance studies demonstrates the tendency to focus on the economic costs of collective action. This emphasis provides an incomplete picture of the calculations made by the decisionmakers in the nations involved in the international situation. Evaluations of these calculations must also include some aspects of the political costs of alliance cooperation.

When we deal with security policy decisions that are the result of both national and international political processes, comparative advantage must incorporate a notion of the political forces that constrain the choices available to decisionmakers in their domestic situations.

Political comparative advantage is largely determined by the domestic political agenda in an alliance nation. The particulars of an ally's domestic political culture create production advantages that differ from those of other allies, because no two polities support identical mixes of policy instruments. In any nation, whether democratic or authoritarian, national security decisionmakers face limited policy choices. These limits are produced by the desires and power of the constituencies they serve. To remain in power, decisionmakers must maintain a coalition of the constituencies that have supported them in the past or develop new coalitions.

If decisionmakers actively work to maintain their support, their policy choices will reflect a responsiveness to constituent interests. In the alliance context, this responsiveness might take the form of military spending if the public supports such spending. In the same country, a leader may be reluctant to adopt the domestic economic measures required to correct international economic imbalances if such policies would have direct negative effects on important constituencies. In countries where opposition to military spending exists but where general alliance goals are supported, economic contributions, such as foreign aid or trade concessions, or political contributions, such as accepting military deployments in the face of negative international pressure, might be the security contributions of choice (or of mandate).[6]

For example, strong and repeated statements by German Chancellor Helmut Kohl regarding the need for a unified Germany to remain within NATO, even in the face of Soviet statements on German unification, were political contributions to Western solidarity. These statements assuaged the fears of Germany's Western neighbors and helped preserve the central role played by the United States in forming the European political landscape during the post–World War II era. They also helped dissipate Soviet fears of an independent, resurgent Germany, thus increasing Western security by decreasing the Soviet's perceived security threats. Political costs within the alliance occur when a nation accepts military deployment (such as with the dual-track decision of 1979 and its deployment in 1983) that supports alliance goals but that is not widely supported domestically. Alliance membership itself can be a cost, particularly when it means subordinating short-term political considerations to the broader security goals of the alliance. Allied economic and military support for the 1990–91 American-led initiative against Iraq is a case in point, given the oil dependence and fears of terrorism that existed in Europe.

Political constraints are not the only sources of comparative advantage in the present context; traditional economic concepts of comparative advantage also influence national decisions regarding alliance contributions. The different national endowments of the factors of production, such as land, labor, capital, and technology, affect the shape of national production frontiers and specialization. In the production of military goods, economies of scale can be obtained by nations producing large amounts of military goods (see, for instance, Hoag, 1967).[7] For example, it might be cheaper on a per unit basis for a nation to produce a thousand armored personnel carriers than only 20. As for economic security tools, Stanley Sloan (1985b:87–89) argued that nations with colonial histories might well be more efficient foreign aid donors than those without colonial histories, because of cultural, historical, and linguistic affinities between donor and recipient nations. Former colonial powers might also obtain more private benefits from foreign aid than noncolonial powers would because of their ties with their former colony. Former colonial powers, therefore, also might donate larger foreign aid sums than other alliance nations, along the lines posited by Sandler's joint product model of public goods production. Public support (or nonsupport) for research and development or macroeconomic policy changes might make certain nations more efficient producers of these alliance goods.

In essence, both the political and economic sources of comparative advantage provide for specialization in collective action situations where more than one public good is important. The comparative advantages possessed by individual alliance nations give these nations reasons to contribute to multiple public goods in specialized ways. In an alliance, this may mean that some nations devote large amounts of resources to military spending while spending little on foreign aid or doing little to promote international monetary stability. Other nations may find the political and economic costs of military spending prohibitive and, therefore, devote their energies and resources to economic contributions.

Following the logic of international trade theory (and also that of the models in the two appendixes) specialization and the simultaneous intra-alliance trade of public goods will yield more collective welfare than nonspecialized production will yield.[8] Specialization and trade along comparative advantage lines push the alliance security provision outcome closer to the Pareto optimal frontier. This means that allied proposals to increase contributions by all alliance members to a particular contribution category may be counterproductive for alliance security and solidarity and for optimal public goods outcomes. Alliances should encourage contributions by individual members on the comparative advantages possessed by those members. This will have the dual result of pushing production outcomes closer to optimal solutions and of committing the alliance to explicit considerations of multiple goods in its security calculations. Chapter 4 focuses on the application of political comparative advantage to the Western alliance system.

The Nonconsultation Assumption

Alliances, joined freely, are by nature cooperative. This conception of alliance affairs runs counter, though, to the results of studies based on the assumption that decisions are made by alliance members without consideration of the decisions made by others in the alliance. But the intra-alliance consultation within the Western alliance (and within many other collectives, for that matter), defies this assumption. I will assume that some level of cooperation exists among the allies and that this cooperation will be evident in the provision of public goods.[9]

The model in appendix B shows that, when assuming rational consultation among allies, allies will rectify the suboptimal tendencies of public goods provision that may occur soon after alliance formation. This follows the simple logic that, if alliances form to augment power and security, these same nations will try to obtain the full benefits of alliance cooperation. This process is significantly aided by consultation and negotiation among allies, in an effort to coordinate policies and spread the burdens of security throughout the collective.

Richard Cornes and Todd Sandler (1984b) have explored the possibility that members of a community providing a public good do not take as given the level of contribution by other members of the community. They compare this possibility with an independent adjustment, or Nash-Cournot, process, that assumes that one individual's contribution does not provoke a response in the rest of the community (368). When actors exhibit Nash-Cournot behavior, they make decisions and act in a rational, self-interested way without regard for how others will respond to that behavior or will behave themselves. Such is the assumption of the simple public goods model. Nash-Cournot behavior is a competitive, collective, allocation process and is contrasted to a cooperative, or Lindahl, allocation process (McGuire and Groth, 1985:915). A further way of distinguishing between the two resource allocation processes is to consider a Nash-Cournot process as rational, self-interested behavior and a Lindahl process as rational, collectively interested behavior.

If, however, nations do respond to the contribution given by other allies, and if these conjectures are positive (i.e., one individual's contribution provokes others to increase contributions), public good provision will be closer to a Pareto optimal outcome than in the Nash case (and may go beyond a Pareto level). The opposite is true if the conjectures are negative (Cauley, Sandler, and Cornes, 1986:165).[10]

The simple public goods model with zero conjectural variations requires that the analyst believe that alliance nations make their security and spending decisions without considering their impact on other alliance members. One nation must believe that the others in the group will do their part even if it does not. The model also assumes that any alliance spending goal—such as the 1978 NATO long-term defense program or the Development Assistance Committee's foreign aid pledge of 0.7 percent of GDP—are sculpted for public consumption and are not taken seriously by alliance members. Granted, not all alliance members will live up to these collective goals, but they are nonetheless benchmarks for security expenditures and reflect collective sentiment.

Assuming that allies are concerned about what the other members will do and that some common concerns exist, the next step is to factor positive conjectural variations into the alliance model. One cannot neglect intra-alliance peer pressure when it comes to spending decisions. An examination of any major alliance decision since 1945—from German rearmament, to flexible response, to inter-German affairs and conventional arms control—shows the degree to which some allies are consulted and cajoled by other allies in an effort to build alliance solidarity. Moreover, such consultation and pressure exists across the security policy categories and not just in one policy forum.

A permanent alliance framework also has the longer-run effect of lowering transaction costs for alliance decisionmaking, because over time, personal relationships are developed among negotiators and the forums for consultation become institutionalized and take the place of ad hoc, crisis-oriented groups. These developments enhance the predictability of the behavior of the major actors in the alliance and are particularly important in a world system where anarchy otherwise defines international interactions. Any permanent framework that

decreases the costliness of assembling actors for negotiation and facilitates longer-term commitments to the collective aids the pursuit of
international cooperation (Sandler and Cauley, 1977:260–63; Keohane, 1984:89–92; Wagner, 1983:345).

As transaction costs are lowered among the allies, which naturally
occurs over time and a succession of agreements (Axelrod, 1984),
cooperation becomes the standard pattern. In Robert Keohane's
terms, the alliance framework or regime produces economies of scale
that make it less and less costly over time to obtain agreement among
members (1984, 89–90). This is not only a result of the succession
of agreements or iteration in the prisoner's dilemma, public goods
setting.[11] It is also a result of the fact that, as the nations of an alliance
continue to work together, they obtain greater information about the
decisionmaking processes and policies of their allies and also about
their allies' future bargaining positions. In essence, the continual alliance consultation process decreases the uncertainty and risks that
nations face when making decisions about whether or not to cooperate
with other nations (93–94).

The effects of continuing interactions on the prospects for cooperation are also supported by the findings of Robert Axelrod (1984) in
his prisoner's dilemma tournaments, where he found that reciprocated
cooperation and repeated play can induce cooperation among rational
egoistic actors.[12] In short, the ability of actors to build reputations
for cooperation, reliability—and for that matter, for retaliation for
noncooperation—aids in solidifying the more cooperative aspects of
enduring institutions, such as those engendered by Western alliance
relationships. Thomas Borcherding (1981:34–35) summed this up for
the alliance setting by asserting that decisionmaking within alliances
exhibits relatively low transaction costs and that "the 'true' interaction
process probably lies somewhere between cooperative and independent adjustment [Nash] games."[13]

Members of a collective that has had common interests over time
and succeeds in its efforts develop an obligation to contribute to the
collective effort. In the simple public goods case, where only one round
of decisionmaking takes place, it is hard to imagine a sense of obligation
developing. In the Western alliance context, this means that members
are willing to contribute to alliance security because of dues that must
be paid or responsibilities that must be borne as a member of the elite
industrialized democracies, or the Western Club.[14]

Over time, and through consultation and the mounting success of
cooperative efforts, international actors may learn about the value of
cooperation in international affairs (Keohane, 1984:132). In highly
interdependent relationships such as those within the Western alliance

system, policymakers may realize that they can benefit from cooperation and coordination in the pursuit of multidimensional security. Go-it-alone strategies can become counterproductive in the face of the constraints imposed by interdependence.

Nonetheless, studies have yielded conflicting evidence on whether the Western allies exhibit a cooperative (or Lindahl) public goods allocation process for military expenditure. In a study based on Martin McGuire and C. H. Groth's (1985) models of public goods allocation, Glenn Palmer (1989:13–14) found some evidence that a cooperative resource allocation process has become more prominent among the European members of the alliance; but he also found that a number of countries exhibit self-interested behavior regarding their defense expenditure. In a later study, Palmer (1990) also found a mix of cooperative and noncooperative behavior within the alliance but concluded that the allies were more concerned with long-term commitments to the alliance than with short-term economic gains. John Oneal (1990b) also found evidence that the European allies are more cooperative than the alliance as a whole, indicating the strength of integration effects in building a sense of common long-term goals among Europeans.[15] Todd Sandler and James Murdoch (1990), however, saw no evidence of cooperative behavior for ten NATO allies during the period 1961–84 and concluded that the allies make their decisions primarily with short-term self-interest in mind.

So although these studies appear to validate the findings of Olson and Zeckhauser and others, none of them took the analysis beyond military contributions.[16] In particular, efficiency in a one-dimensional environment was difficult to achieve. But when additional goods are added to the security equation, there is a greater possibility for alliance nations to find common interest. Therefore, the free-rider conclusions of these alliance studies, given the broader substantive nature of actual alliance security partnerships, are suspect.

Summing up the Theoretical Critique: Whence the Free-Rider Problem?

By bringing any one of the assumptions of the simple public goods model closer to real-world approximations, one derives hypotheses that question the degree of suboptimality posited by that model's formulators. If we put these assumptions into an integrated framework where they all work together, possibly synergistically, we find an even stronger argument for the potential for international cooperation. Thus we can conclude that the free-rider problem as outlined in chapter 2 is overstated and perhaps nonexistent. The belief that international actors cannot act in concert in the face of forces that promote collective action can only be based on ignorance of the ways nation-states interact in contemporary international affairs. This statement carries even more weight when we consider the fact that members of a noncoercive alliance share common security policy goals. Given these facts, we should be surprised if cooperation and the provision of public goods are *not* achieved.

Although we cannot conclude that alliance security provision will be optimal, we can state that security provision will be closer to optimality when alliance nations specialize in the security contributions for which they possess comparative advantages. Evaluations of multiple security goods provision would give quite different results than evaluations of alliance efficiency based on only one security dimension. By specializing, alliance nations can capitalize on production advantages and national preferences and make worthwhile contributions to the alliance security effort.

The exact nature of the burden-sharing arrangements that will be made among members of a collective will depend upon the relative bargaining abilities of the individual actors, on the configuration of these actors' preferences, and on what each actor has to offer to the collective. However, any multiple-issue trade will improve the alliance security situation. Additionally, alliance burden-sharing arrangements will not be static but will change over time. Given the nature of the political process in most liberal democracies, these changes will likely evolve gradually. As a country's political sentiments and economic priorities shift, so will its specific contributions. For example, the American role as guarantor of international economic stability gave way to domestic economic and political priorities in the late 1960s and early 1970s. As American economic preeminence was increasingly challenged by allied economic redevelopment and strength, America increasingly demanded that the allies pull their weight, at least economically. Thus the interdependencies that tie an alliance together also force it to adapt to change by shifting the collective arrangements.

The preceding analysis complements past work by Russett, Sandler, and others by demonstrating yet another force that causes alliance nations to help provide alliance security. The incentives of the private benefits of security contributions and the tendencies toward specialization push alliance security provision closer to an efficient outcome. When free riding is identified in the alliance context, the analyst should examine other alliance contributions to discover the specialization of the apparent free rider. Free riding is less likely the norm and more likely an indication that specialization and trade of public goods is occurring.[17] Given the way the Western alliance system actually works, it is not surprising that the alliance has endured and that it has achieved many of its goals. Its success is based on a commonality of security interests, continual consultation, and the production of numerous public and private goods that serve its multidimensional security interests.

4

Political Comparative Advantage

YUKIO SATOH (1982) claimed that "Japanese security policy will inevitably be different from that pursued by the United States or by other major industrialized nations of the West, although a broad identity of policy objectives with Western nations will be maintained. . . . Japan's individual features can be turned to the advantage of the West provided they are recognized and translated" (40). Gregory Flynn (1981) thought that, although basic objectives "will often be identical," the "problem will be to make sure that external security does not suffer at the hands of allies attempting to maintain maximum policy flexibility in the absence of a common hierarchy of priorities" (181). Stanley Sloan (1985b) believed that "many Europeans fear . . . an American tendency to concentrate too narrowly on military responses to potential Soviet aggression. . . . They are at least equally . . . interested in developing economic ties and political bonds . . . with the Third World nations" (88).

These passages suggest that Western alliance nations have possessed a core of security objectives: (1) containment of Soviet influence in the world, (2) perpetuation of a stable and open international economy, and (3) domestic and international political stability. All of these are, in varying degrees, public goods. Each passage points, as well, to differences within the alliance regarding the means to pursue these common objectives. Each nation naturally, has a different hierarchy of preferred policy tools and also has other private objectives aside from the collective's security concerns. But although such differences can divide the alliance, the Satoh passage suggests that they can also strengthen alliance security by focusing on the positive exploitation of divergent policy preferences (and variations in the intensity with which these preferences are held). This chapter examines both the common and the divergent preferences within the alliance as they pertain to multiple-issue security cooperation and to the distribution of burdens borne by alliance members.

Western nations have increasingly considered nonmilitary problems important to their security calculations, both domestically and within the alliance context.[1] Moreover, one study found that even in the United States, where strong support for military spending continues, nearly 60 percent of the respondents felt "that threats to our national security are changing, and that these new threats require different kinds of national policies than the ones the United States has relied upon in the past" (Martilla, 1989:266).[2] Since alliance nations increasingly define security in more than military terms, and since the security utility functions of individual allies are defined across multiple alliance goods, evaluations of alliance security must also consider the provision of goods other than military defense.[3]

This chapter moves toward such comprehensive analyses of security cooperation by examining the many security preferences within the Western alliance. This endeavor is based at the theoretical level on the assumptions of international trade theory that policy constraints produce conditions that can facilitate a division of labor among the allies regarding alliance security. These political comparative advantages can promote alliance contribution specialization and, ultimately, produce more efficient alliance security provision. Such concepts as political comparative advantage and multidimensional burden sharing spring from a divergence of national priorities and objectives. These divergencies can be turned to the advantage of the alliance if exploited in a productive manner and not seen as lack of commitment to collective strategies and goals.

The concept of political comparative advantage springs from the requisite political responsiveness of national elites in Western political systems. Political responsiveness and the bounded policymaking process it implies can be examined through the use of public opinion data on security issues. Although policymakers will not always follow the will of the people because of its apparent volatility, we should be able to see in broad outline the constraints confronting Western national security policymakers and the policy tools that are available to them.[4]

From a policy perspective, an examination of security policy preferences can result in alliance burden-sharing strategies that exploit political comparative advantages rather than demand across-the-board spending increases in all expenditure categories. As Richard Cheney (1989) has noted regarding the NATO 3 percent real growth goal for defense spending (52), some nations have been unwilling or unable to increase this type of spending and should thus be encouraged to devote resources to the areas where they are politically able to do so. If we understand the policy constraints in each Western alliance nation, we can fine-tune policy initiatives to focus on the particular security policy tools that will increase alliance security.

Some Conceptual and Methodological Concerns

Before I move to the empirical analysis, a number of conceptual and methodological concerns should be addressed. A first point relates to Joe Oppenheimer's (1979) criticism of the application of public goods theory (and its associated rational actor viewpoint) to problems of international politics. As he suggested, the assumption that nation-states are the primary decisionmaking units in the international system may lead to conceptual errors regarding hypotheses about the ability of nation-states to cooperate effectively (396–98). In many respects, this argument echoes that made by Graham Allison (1971) against the rational unitary-actor model of national decisionmaking.

Policy decisions are often the result of parochial concerns within a government system rather than rational evaluations of economic efficiency. Drawing on a wide and varied literature, Oppenheimer (1979) enumerated the problems associated with such group decisions (cyclical outcomes in voting theory and the suboptimality theorem of public goods theory).[5] He suggested that, to assume that nations are rational utility maximizers internationally implies that these collectives have produced a Pareto-optimal result at the national level (395–96). Theoretical inconsistency as obvious as this requires that we take a much closer look at the assumptions of public goods theories as applied to international cooperation.

One can respond to Oppenheimer's criticism, as Todd Sandler, Jon Cauley, and John Forbes (1980:542–44) did, by stating that the utility maximizers in the international realm are national decisionmakers. This also suggests that, to understand national utility maximization, one must investigate the decisionmaking and electoral structures of the nation-states in question. By answering Oppenheimer's criticism in this way, we can begin to understand the political dimension of comparative advantage and how it affects the ways nations allocate resources to alliance security concerns.[6] For instance, if a particular policy choice would result in loss of office for a decisionmaker, that choice will not be found on or within the boundaries of a nation's production function. This is analogous to saying—in a purely economic context—that if a firm has the raw materials to produce only twenty tractors per year, it cannot choose to produce twenty-five tractors per year. Obviously, then, the policy decisions discussed in this chapter rule out political suicide. True, the outcomes of policy decisions are often unknown, as evidenced by the myriad political miscalculations that occur in any political system, but in the present context, it is assumed that conscious disregard of the political dimensions of the national production constraint does not occur.

Other conceptual limitations to the following analysis should also be mentioned before we move on to the main tasks of this chapter. First, the data discussed below are on mass attitudes and not on those of the opinion leaders in Western alliance countries. Thus this chapter examines the potential constraints on decisionmakers rather than their actual preferences. In addition, the intensity of these opinions is not examined. Thus, one runs the risk of examining only the views of a silent majority and not those of a potentially vociferous and important, even if small, minority (Flynn and Rattinger, 1985:3–4). Unfortunately, data for opinion leaders are much more difficult to come by; one thus must make conjectures from data once removed from the source of interest. By breaking the data down along educational and age lines, one can also get a more direct reading of opinion leader attitudes, but this reading is limited by data availability and suffers from decreased sample size.

Second, the following analysis does not suggest that definitive answers can be obtained regarding the security preferences of Western alliance countries. Rather, it tries to highlight both the commonalities and the differences within the alliance. The patterns change over time, but changing patterns can lead the alliance to adapt to new challenges to its security concerns and do not necessarily lead to alliance disintegration. This adaptability will likely be tested in the 1990s and beyond, given the changes in Eastern Europe and the former Soviet Union, especially as they relate to the intensity of the military threat perceived by Western alliance countries.

Third, the use of opinion polling implies that respondents will truthfully reveal their preferences regarding security policy choices. One of the principal reasons public goods are hypothesized as being provided at suboptimal levels is because public goods are joint and nonexcludable. Therefore, individuals have incentives to lie about their demand for a public good. If the individual reveals his or her true demand, he or she will be expected to pay that share (the marginal rate of substitution) of the cost of the public good. But if the individual purposely underestimates his or her true demand, he or she is still able to consume the good if it is provided for any individual, thereby free riding on those who reveal more demand.

Some skepticism about the validity of public opinion results is therefore warranted, particularly as they relate to questions of public goods. On the other hand, a variety of experimental studies of the free-rider problem have found that individuals are more inclined to reveal their demand for a public good than is expected by the theoretical constructs of public goods analysis (Bohm, 1972; Marwell and Ames, 1979, 1980, 1981; Alfano and Marwell, 1981; Sweeney, 1973; and Scherr and Babb, 1975).

Alliance Nations' Commitment to Security Issues

It is useful to recognize how committed alliance nations have been to alliance relationships. Table 4.1 shows that, in each country listed, a large degree of support existed for NATO, support that did not change much between 1967 and 1989. Not surprisingly, France, with its penchant for an independent course, showed the most ambivalence regarding the need for NATO, although there appeared to be an upswing in support in later years. Even so, French opinion has always shown at least a plurality supporting NATO.

Although asked a somewhat different question, the American public's commitment to NATO has been as strong as that of its European partners, demonstrating that throughout the alliance a large degree of solidarity has existed with reference to NATO's course (see table 4.2). Gregory Flynn and Hans Rattinger (1985:375) also found that NATO publics believed "that NATO is the best way to organize security," even though the publics did not believe that NATO policies were necessarily the best ways to pursue security. William Domke, Richard Eichenberg, and Catherine Kelleher (1987) and David Capitanchik and Eichenberg (1983) reached similar conclusions. Capitanchik and Eichenberg suggested (80, 86–87) that labeling European public sentiments in the early 1980s as *neutralism* is too simple.

Differences do exist, however, among NATO publics in their attitudes toward security and defense. Table 4.3 shows the variation in the issues deemed important in nine NATO nations. Some of the differences break down along regional lines; others do not. First, a high unemployment rate was the most important issue in each nation except Japan. This is not surprising considering the economic slump of the early 1980s and the dates the surveys were taken. The United States, however, should not be lumped with the seven European countries registering high marks on this issue. Although unemployment was the most important issue for the United States in these surveys, it was a much stronger concern for the Europeans. This may have resulted from the quicker American economic recovery in the 1980s

TABLE 4.1
Allied Commitment to NATO: Is NATO Still Essential?

	UK		FR		WG		IT		BE		DE		NE	
Year	Yes	No	Yes	No	Yes	No	Yes	No	Yes	No	Yes	No	Yes	No
1967	59	15	34	30	67	17								
1969	68	15	47	37	76	13	66	23						
1971	81	12	54	35	84	11								
1973			42	34	73	13								
1976	69	15	42	35	85	10	58	30						
1977	73	08	44	29	79	07	54	24					78	11
1978	70	10	39	35	84	05	58	22			62	16	71	10
1980	79	13	44	34	88	08	54	25	56	20			63	26
1981	70	15			62	20	62	27					62	15
1982	65	25	34	26	66	18	55	31					67	16
1983	72	16			86	12	61	26						
1984	76	12			87	10	63	24	60	20	63	19	58	20
1987[a]	72	17	49	28	71	11	58	29						
1987[b]	72	16	48	19	70	15	65	23			61	22		
1988	72	17	58	22	76	13	53	31	66	22	70	23	64	25
1989	67	17	41	28	59	24	46	28	55	30	68	24	58	30

Sources: Based on "Opinion Roundup" (1989:21); Domke, Eichenberg, and Kelleher (1987:386); Commission of the European Communities (1989).

Notes: "Don't know" answers are not listed but can be derived by adding percentages and subtracting from 100.

Values are given as percentages.

[a]February.

[b]September except for Denmark, which was surveyed in October.

Abbreviations: UK, United Kingdom; FR, France; WG, West Germany; IT, Italy; BE, Belgium; DE, Denmark; NE, The Netherlands.

relative to its European counterparts, making unemployment a more intense concern in Europe (Fitoussi and Phelps, 1986).

Inflation was accorded lower priority than unemployment in each nation except Japan, where it was more important than unemployment. Respondents in France, Italy, and the United States showed the greatest concern over this issue; Japan was a somewhat distant fourth. The lower priority of inflation is not surprising given the tendency for lower inflation rates during times of recession.

Some interesting facts also emerge from this table regarding military issues. First, respondents in all the countries accorded some concern to the threat of war, with the highest threat perceived by Italians. In addition, except for high unemployment, the threat of war received the highest values on average across the nine nations.[7] This issue can be put into perspective by examining it in tandem with the issue of insufficient defense capability. Only in the United States did a

TABLE 4.2
American Commitment to NATO

Year	Increase or keep commitment	Decrease or end commitment	Don't know
1974	54	20	26
1978	67	13	20
1982	67	15	18
1986	70	16	14

Sources: Based on Domke, Eichenberg, and Kelleher (1987:387); "Opinion Roundup" (1989:30).

Notes: To the question, Would you agree or disagree that NATO is still necessary for the defense of Western Europe? 79 percent answered "necessary" and 15 percent answered "not necessary." See *ABC News/Washington Post* poll (1989).

Values are given as percentages.

substantial number of respondents find defense capability an important issue.[8] (Table 4.4 provides a greater insight into allied support for military spending.)

A number of other patterns can be seen in table 4.3. First, nuclear weapons, not surprisingly, were a major concern, perhaps reflecting the high visibility of nuclear weapons issues in general but, more specifically, the deployment of the Pershing II and ground-launched cruise missiles in the fall of 1983, coinciding with the time these surveys were taken. There was also a dramatic decline between 1983 and 1984 in the number of West German respondents citing nuclear weapons as an important issue. Second, the energy crisis was of greatest importance for Japanese respondents because of the dependence of Japan on oil imports. (The United States and Italy also showed some concern over this issue.) Third, excessive government deficits were also an important issue for a number of countries, notably the United States.

From this table, we can make some general conjectures about the political comparative advantages possessed by various alliance nations, most strikingly regarding defense capability and threat of war results. As table 4.4 shows, throughout the early 1980s, American support for increases in defense spending was much higher than that in Europe. And even though support for increases tailed off by mid-decade, support for maintenance of the Reagan era defense budgets continued until the late 1980s. Although pluralities of European respondents favored current levels of military spending, none except possibly Great Britain exhibited the upward pressure shown in the United States. Great Britain tended to spend relatively more on defense than most other Western allies.[9] These findings also support the Olson and Zeck-

TABLE 4.3
The Most Important Issues to Alliance Countries, 1983, 1984

Issue	FR 1983	FR 1984	WG 1983	WG 1984	UK 1983	UK 1984	IT 1983	IT 1984	NE 1983	NW 1983	NW 1984	US 1983	US 1984	J 1983	J 1984	SP 1984
Threat of war	44	47	28	14	31	40	55	56	37	36	30	45	32	42	35	49
Energy crisis	14	15	14	4	5	15	22	19	9	2	1	23	7	26	24	13
Inflation	46	39	16	9	21	18	41	38	10	7	3	38	30	29	26	23
Insufficient defense capability	5	7	8	2	7	11	7	7	5	6	4	24	10	10	9	5
High unemployment rate	76	78	73	52	61	60	72	69	70	66	64	46	36	22	16	85
Unfairness, inequality	26	27	24	12	14	23	30	28	19	17	15	24	13	27	26	32
Crime	27	30	34	10	37	36	56	58	47	16	12	44	30	33	34	34
Nuclear weapons	26	26	38	15	29	43	35	39	49	38	31	37	28	34	32	33
Excessive government deficit	20	21	25	5	9	12	22	19	17	6	4	37	26	21	21	13
Poor political leadership	24	24	15	7	16	19	27	25	19	11	9	35	21	22	16	4
Other or no answer	1	2	9	5	2	1	4	3	6	4	3	3	4	11	11	

Sources: Based on Hastings and Hastings (1986:718–19, 1987:689).
Notes: The question was, What is the most important issue for you and for your country at the present time?
Values are given as percentages.
Abbreviations: FR, France; WG, West Germany; UK, United Kingdom; IT, Italy; NE, The Netherlands; NW, Norway; US, United States; J, Japan; SP, Spain.

TABLE 4.4
Alliance Countries' Desired Level of Defense Spending, 1980s

Country	Increase spending	Decrease spending	Keep spending at present level	Don't know
United Kingdom				
1980	30	10	47	7
1981	33	15	44	8
1982	44	16	36	4
1984	23	20	52	5
1987	17	27	49	7
France				
1980	4	32	38	25
1981	15	24	49	1
1982	16	24	55	5
1987	9	35	45	11
West Germany				
1980	22	19	53	17
1981	15	20	50	15
1982	15	26	43	16
1984	7	33	58	2
1987	4	57	39	
Italy				
1980	10	39	36	15
1981	16	43	36	6
1982	16	46	34	4
1984	18	42	34	6
1987	8	62	22	8
Netherlands				
1981	11	36	35	17
1984	8	29	49	14
Norway				
1981	21	16	52	11
1984	30	21	26	23
Denmark				
1984	14	22	53	11
Belgium				
1984	7	37	46	10
United States				
1980	71	6	21	2
1981	58	16	22	4
1982	43	18	37	2
1983	28	20	47	5
1985	14	32	52	2
1987	22	28	49	1
1988	14	31	53	2
1990	3	53	42	2

Sources: Based on U.S. International Communications Agency (1982); U.S. Information Agency (1984); Hastings and Hastings (1988:610, 1987:300, 1990:261).
Note: Values are given as percentages.

hauser notion that the small exploit the large in terms of contributions to alliance military defense, although this dichotomy does not carry over to opinions on other policy instruments.

An aversion to increased defense spending is also shown in Japanese data. The following questions were asked of the Japanese public in 1985 (Hastings and Hastings, 1987:300, 1986:326, 1990:168).

The government has had a policy of maintaining defense spending at less than 1 percent of gross national product. However, under the Defense Reorganization Five-Year Program adopted by the Nakasone cabinet, the total defense expenditure is expected to exceed slightly 1 percent of GNP. What do you think of this plan?

Oppose because it ignores the 1 percent limit.	21%
Approve because the excess is slight.	29%
Defense expenditure should be increased regardless of past limits.	6%
Defense expenditures should be decreased.	31%
Other or no answer.	13%

If the defense budget continues to increase, it may exceed the 1 percent of the GNP in spite of the government's policy. What do you think about this?

Should keep it within 1 percent.	43%
Exceeding 1 percent may be inevitable.	16%
Should increase beyond 1 percent.	3%
Defense budget should be greatly decreased.	23%
Don't know or no answer.	15%

In 1987 and 1988, the following questions were asked: What do you think should be done (if anything) to our self-defense army's capability? (1987). Choose the one opinion among the following which most closely represents your opinion of the Self-Defense Forces (1988).

	1987	1988
Should be increased.	8%	8%
Should remain the same.	63%	67%
Should be reduced.	18%	17%
Should be eliminated.	4%	3%
Other or don't know.	7%	5%

As American opinions on defense spending suggest, much of the defense buildup decided upon by the alliance in the late 1970s was supported by the American public and was largely carried out by American spending.[10] Thus the United States put its political comparative advantage to good use by devoting resources to strongly supported spending categories serving alliance security interests at the time that the allies were politically unable to make such allocations.

Allied security perceptions and requirements can also be gleaned from public attitudes toward foreign aid. Development assistance spending is a security policy tool, since it promotes a positive alliance image in the world; it also serves the economic interests of the alliance by contributing to economic prosperity and stability in out-of-area regions. Tables 4.5, 4.6, and 4.7 show the attitudes of the allies toward development assistance. Public support for foreign aid in Italy was quite high, especially in 1980. Support for foreign aid was also strong in Luxembourg, Denmark, the Netherlands, Canada, and Greece, and French opinion also tended to be supportive. The United Kingdom, Belgium, and West Germany, however, exhibited somewhat lower support. It is difficult to know what to attribute these variances to other than ideology. The welfare state is an entrenched part of the political system in Luxembourg, Denmark, and the Netherlands, but what then accounts for the low degree of support in the United Kingdom, Belgium and West Germany? More refined opinion measures are needed to thoroughly evaluate European attitudes in this policy area.

The attitudes of Americans become clearer when we combine the results of the 1981 question with the data in table 4.8. This table also shows American opposition to foreign aid increases: while the defense budget was generally supported during the 1973–90 period, foreign aid spending was widely opposed.[11] This opposition is reflected in the relatively low percentage of GDP that the United States has traditionally devoted to foreign aid and also fits with the substantial postwar military buildups under Truman, Kennedy, Carter, and Reagan.

The opinions of the Japanese on defense and aid were surveyed in 1984 (Hastings and Hastings, 1986:328). The following question was asked: One of the United States' requests for Japan's increased defense capability is that Japan should cover a thousand-mile sea-lane outside of Japan; have you heard of this request?

Have heard.	37%
Have not heard.	58%
No answer.	5%

Respondents indicating they had heard were asked, Which one of the following opinions on sea-lane defense do you agree with?

It is necessary for Japan's security and continued access to natural resources.	33%
It is currently impossible because the defense plan requires a large increase in Japan's defense capability.	14%

TABLE 4.5
Alliance Countries' Desired Level of Aid to Developing Countries, 1980

Opinion	BE	CA	DE	FR	UK	IT	LU	NE	WG
Increased aid	14	25	15	31	13	58	36	16	16
Keep aid at present level	40	40	42	43	36	24	47	61	54
Decrease aid	34	28	33	18	45	7	13	28	20

Source: Based on Gallup Political Index (1980).
Notes: The question was, Now I would like to ask if you think that our aid to the developing countries should be increased, remain the same, or decrease. Italians were asked, Now I would like to ask if you think that aid to the developing countries should be increased, remain the same, or decreased.
Values are given as percentages.
Abbreviations: BE, Belgium; *CA,* Canada; *DE,* Denmark; *FR,* France; *UK,* United Kingdom; *IT,* Italy; *LU,* Luxembourg; *NE,* The Netherlands; *WG,* West Germany.

TABLE 4.6
Alliance Countries' Desired Level of Aid to Developing Countries, 1981

Opinion	Canada	United States	West Germany	United Kingdom
Increase aid	51	32	35	35
Don't increase aid	37	60	64	58
Don't know	12	8	1	8

Source: Based on Gallup Political Index (1981).
Notes: The question was, Do you feel that [country name] should or should not increase aid to underdeveloped countries to assist them to become self-sufficient in the future.
Values are given as percentages.

> Security should be maintained by diplomacy and economic
> cooperation, rather than military measures. Therefore,
> I am against the defense plan.   46%
> Other.   1%
> No answer.   6%

Building on the diplomacy and economic cooperation result of this question, the Japanese were queried in 1986 and 1987 on foreign aid, which they call *economic cooperation* (Hastings and Hastings, 1989:195–96, 1990:42). The questions began, Developed countries are cooperating economically with developing countries by providing capital and cooperating on technology. Taking into consideration a variety of perspectives, do you think that Japan should continue to increase its active economic cooperation or not? (1986). Developed nations give economic

TABLE 4.7
Alliance Countries' Willingness to Sacrifice
1 Percent of Salaries to Aid Developing Countries, 1983

Opinion	BE	DE	WG	FR	IT	LU	NE	UK	GR
Agree to give up 1% of salary	39	59	34	48	69	67	63	46	72
Do not agree	46	27	42	45	24	24	27	44	24
No reply	15	14	24	7	7	9	10	10	4

Source: Based on Hastings and Hastings (1986:667).
Notes: The question was, If you were told that in order to give more help to Third World countries it would be necessary to hold back 1 percent from your salary, would you agree to this idea or not.
Values are given as percentages.
Abbreviations: BE, Belgium; *DE,* Denmark; *WG,* West Germany; *FR,* France; *IT,* Italy; *LU,* Luxembourg; *NE,* The Netherlands; *UK,* United Kingdom; *GR,* Greece.

aid to developing nations in the form of financial assistance and technical cooperation. Do you think Japan should continue to give economic aid to developing nations in an active manner in the future? (1987).

	1986	1987
Should continue at increased level (1987). Should become more active (1986).	39%	38%
Should continue at present level.	42%	42%
Should reduce level (1987). Should decrease activity (1986).	8%	8%
Should stop entirely.	1%	2%
Don't know.	10%	10%

It seems from the foregoing that the Japanese prefer that security be maintained through diplomacy and economic cooperation rather than military means. It is also clear that respondents favored economic cooperation. Japan most likely possessed a political advantage in alliance burden sharing in the economic realm, which follows from published policy statements and from analyses of the Japanese policy of comprehensive security (Bobrow, 1984; Chapman, Drifte, and Gow, 1982; and Satoh, 1982). Moreover, the Japanese government has the political capital to devote to increased foreign aid donations. In interviews, Japanese officials indicated that the Japanese government believes foreign aid spending produces higher security returns per yen than does military spending.[12]

So the data suggest that Italy, Japan, Denmark, the Netherlands, Luxembourg, Canada, and Greece were better equipped at least politi-

TABLE 4.8
American Attitudes toward Foreign Aid and
Defense Spending, 1973–1990

Spending category	Too little	About right	Too much	Don't know
Foreign aid				
1973	4	20	70	5
1974	3	17	76	4
1975	5	17	73	5
1976	3	18	75	4
1977	3	24	66	7
1978	4	24	67	6
1980	5	20	70	5
1982	5	18	72	5
1983	4	17	74	5
1984	4	21	70	5
1985	7	24	65	4
1986	6	19	71	4
1987	7	20	69	4
1988	5	22	68	5
1989	4	22	68	6
1990	5	24	66	5
Military armaments and defense				
1973	11	45	38	6
1974	17	45	31	7
1975	17	46	31	7
1976	24	42	27	7
1977	24	45	23	8
1978	27	44	22	8
1980	50	26	11	6
1982	29	36	30	5
1983	24	38	32	6
1984	17	41	38	3
1985	14	42	40	3
1986	16	38	40	5
1987	15	41	41	4
1988	16	40	38	6
1989	15	41	39	6
1990	10	43	43	5

Source: Based on National Opinion Research Center (1991).
Notes: The question was, We are faced with many problems in this country, none of which can be solved easily or inexpensively. I'm going to name some of these problems, and for each one I'd like you to tell me whether you think we're spending too much money on it, too little money, or about the right amount. First, are we spending too much, too little, or about the right amount on [spending category].
Values are given as percentages.

cally to bear relatively large alliance foreign aid burdens. Moreover, considering that these nations, with the exception of Greece, have been reluctant or unable to increase military spending, foreign aid appears as an alternative, yet potent, way for these nations to contribute to alliance security. Alliance decisionmakers should encourage these countries to capitalize on their apparent political advantages and specialize in the foreign aid realm. Because Greece obtains large private benefits from military spending (e.g., defense against Turkey), it possesses yet another mix of preferred policy tools (or a different security utility function).

Contributions to the liberal international economic order should also be examined when we look at the burden-sharing question, since the maintenance of the liberal economic order established after World War II is directly related to the future prosperity and security of alliance nations. The following question was asked of respondents in eight alliance countries: What do you think of the opinion that, although liberalization of trade may result in great benefit, importing goods should be limited in order to prevent worsening of the unemployment situation? (Hastings and Hastings, 1986: 719). The following percentages agreed with the statement, In the short run, unemployment is the most serious for my nation.

France	48
West Germany	39
United Kingdom	53
Italy	53
Netherlands	29
Norway	45
United States	63
Japan	35

The following percentages agreed with the statement, It will worsen the unemployment situation in the long run, because other nations are going to limit imports in revenge. (Don't know or no answers are in parentheses.)

France	40 (12)
West Germany	27 (34)
United Kingdom	36 (11)
Italy	21 (26)
Netherlands	47 (24)
Norway	47 (8)
United States	31 (6)
Japan	33 (32)

As Steven Smith and Douglas Wertman (1989) state, and as is supported by the answers to the question above, although free trade is widely supported in principle, this support breaks down when the question is related to unemployment or the protection of domestic industries (42–43).[13] This tendency occurred throughout the 1980s:

> In a March–April 1983 survey, for example, majorities in Britain, Italy, and the United States and pluralities in France, Japan, and West Germany wanted to "progressively reduce trade restrictions and encourage free international trade" as a means to deal with economic difficulties; in the same battery of questions, however, majorities or pluralities in each of these countries wanted to "protect national producers by increased import restrictions." (43)

Similar anomalies were found in April 1983 and March 1984 surveys. These generalities have been supported by the problems encountered in the Uruguay Round of GATT negotiations, as the European Community and Japan dug in their heels regarding agricultural subsidies.

The differences between the percentages favoring and not favoring protectionist national policies show the degree of political power protectionist sentiment carries.

France	8%
West Germany	12%
United Kingdom	17%
Italy	32%
Netherlands	−18%
Norway	−2%
United States	32%
Japan	2%

A positive percentage indicates strong protectionist orientation, while a negative percentage shows support for liberalization. Percentages approaching zero indicate either a nonissue or a controversy. These figures suggest that the United States and Italy had the strongest protectionist support of the eight countries. The Netherlands shows the strongest support for liberalization.

This survey suggests that the Netherlands can make contributions to alliance security in the form of support for liberalization efforts. Considering the export dependence of this small nation, such an outcome is not surprising, but its domestic political advantage may well be constrained by its participation in the European Community. Depending upon whether or not trade is a controversial domestic issue in Japan and Norway, these nations could also contribute in this way. Since Japan is often labeled a free rider in the military realm and because it relies heavily on export revenues, it might contribute to alliance security by further opening its markets and supporting strong liberalization. Too, such liberalization might promote intra-alliance harmony, since the Japanese have been repeatedly accused of keeping their markets closed. Elites in nations with strong protectionist sentiments may not be as able, politically, to support liberalization efforts, so at least in the short term these nations possess some bargaining power in alliance trade relations because of these political constraints.

It is interesting to note the strong protectionist feelings in the United States, especially in light of the historic American role as supporter and promoter of a liberal international order.[14] Issues of reciprocity are most likely crucial to public perceptions of trade liberalization: where reciprocity is perceived, free trade and the policy choices it entails will likely be supported. As Robert Axelrod and Robert Keohane (1986:249) have suggested cooperation in international relations is "attained best not by providing benefits unilaterally to others, but by conditional cooperation" based on both positive and negative reciprocity. In the case discussed here, this means supporting liberal trade policies when others do and being able to effectively punish overly protectionist nations when the situation warrants. Reciprocity as it applies to trade policies was strongly supported by American respondents when asked questions regarding the alternative trade strategies available to a particular administration.[15]

As for the need for economic policy coordination among the alliance nations, the following question was asked of respondents in six alliance nations: How important do you think it is for the economic health of [our country] to closely coordinate our policies with the United States? (Smith and Wertman, 1989:42). The following percentages thought it was very important or fairly important.

France	63
Italy	66
Britain	58
Germany	56
Canada	79
Japan	84

Considering the increasing cooperation in the Group of Seven's (G-7) negotiations on monetary policy since 1985, it is not surprising that the respondents wanted to coordinate their countries' economic policies with the United States. These results may also bode well for cooperation in the trade realm in the face of the changes brought by the 1992 unification of the European Community. Cooperation will also be aided by an increasingly liberal EC commission ("Europe's

Internal Market," 1989:11). It is somewhat surprising, though, that of the six countries surveyed, Britain and Germany showed the smallest majorities in favor of coordination, as these two are often seen as the most steadfast of the European allies. The two non-EC countries, Japan and Canada, not surprisingly placed the highest value on policy coordination with the United States. Despite the lower support for policy coordination in the EC countries surveyed, these results taken with European attitudes toward NATO (Tables 4.1 and 4.2) indicate that the ties that bind the alliance together are strong. As Gregory Flynn (1981) put it, "disharmony is not necessarily rooted in the objectives, but in the means to accomplish them" (230).

These policy coordination poll results can also be taken as evidence of the degree to which the allies feel that they possess a shared destiny. This interconnectedness, while at times the source of contention, also bodes well for the future of the alliance in that policy coordination leads to increased interdependence and an increased need for cooperation. The cooperative efforts of alliance nations in economic, military, and political realms ultimately leads to a more integrated alliance system. These efforts along with tendencies to specialize in alliance security policies enhance incentives for continued alliance participation. Specialization and division of labor among allies, then, is a positive force in alliance duration.

Conclusions

The data presented in this chapter give an idea of the political constraints confronted by national security decisionmakers and the political comparative advantages these nations possess. Although the political advantages revealed by public opinion do not necessarily reflect the policy choices of the government, in liberal democracies, at least, some responsiveness to the public must be assumed. Thus it is not unrealistic to use the data to conjecture about the present and future pattern of alliance burden sharing and to project alliance policy options. A more complete picture of these advantages and the policy choices they entail can be made only through an examination of data on the actual resources allocated to particular policy tools.

Two other points of clarification are necessary regarding the political advantages revealed above. First, international trade theory, and the hypotheses it suggests regarding comparative advantage and specialization, does not require that nations possess an absolute advantage in the production of a particular good but only a comparative advantage as measured by the opportunity costs of production in that nation.

By extension to the political advantage argument, one only needs to establish that a nation does not have a political advantage in the production of a particular alliance good to identify which good it should produce. If, for example, the United States has a political advantage in military spending, other nations should specialize in the production of other types of alliance security goods, such as foreign aid or contributions to monetary stabilization. Every nation possesses some political comparative advantage and can thus make contributions to the alliance effort.

An investigation of the correlation of national political comparative advantages with economic comparative advantages would allow greater understanding of the future economic health and political stability of particular alliance nations. If a nation is economically advantaged in a certain good's production but politically advantaged in another—and given the political responsiveness of decisionmakers— one could predict economically shortsighted decisions being made for politically farsighted reasons. When political and economic comparative advantages correspond, one can hypothesize that the nation is well situated for economic growth and political stability over the long term.

This argument could be extended to tie in with the argument in Paul Kennedy's *Rise and Fall of the Great Powers* (1987). If, as Kennedy suggested, the United States is tilted toward military expenditures and investment to the detriment of economic health, a comparative advantage in a relatively unproductive economic endeavor (military production) runs counter to national economic health. As a result, the United States has relied on others to help rectify its external imbalances (recently under the G-7 agreements). Further, if the United States continues to exploit its production advantage, it will become increasingly reliant on its allies for economic security goods. Normative evaluations of the prudence of the continuation of this policy are dependent upon assumptions about the likelihood of continuing intra-alliance commonalities and the desirability of increasing intra-alliance reliance and interdependence. This topic is discussed more thoroughly in chapter 7.

As the pieces of times series public opinion data illustrate, political advantages are not static: shifts in public sentiment do occur. American opinions on defense expenditures, for example, show fluctuations. Although somewhat less striking, European opinions on military spending also shifted over time. Thus we should not assume that a nation's political advantage is permanent; advantages and preferences will change over time, thus changing the specialization of the various allies and prompting periodic reevaluations of the patterns of alliance security burdens. But these changes in specialization should be only a matter of adjustment and incremental change rather than fundamental reorganization. Indeed, the forces for change can help the alliance adapt to new challenges and need not contribute to intra-alliance conflict or alliance disintegration.

As I stated previously, the burden-sharing debate within NATO has persistently focused on the military efforts made by the various alliance nations. But this narrow appraisal of alliance security efforts ignores the increasing tendency of alliance nations to define security in nonmilitary ways and also does not examine the policy choices made outside the military sector that also serve security purposes. As a result, analyses of military burden sharing alone capture only a small segment of the alliance security equation.

We must appreciate the diversity of security preferences among nations and the specialization tendencies within the alliance. These differences will not be the roots of conflict and disintegration, and low military spending does not necessarily mean free riding or lack of commitment to the alliance. As Leonard Sullivan (1985) aptly put it: "All valid contributions to the common prosperity must be credited. Most welcome should be those contributions that make effective use of each donor's limited capabilities" (93).

5

Measuring Security Cooperation

Earlier studies of alliance burden sharing have generated two basic hypotheses: (1) alliances do not produce alliance defense efficiently, that is, they produce suboptimal amounts of the public good the alliance desires, and (2) smaller allies tend to free ride on the defense expenditures of larger allies. These hypotheses have been supported by a variety of studies employing diverse data and statistical techniques. But with few exceptions, analyses of Western alliance security cooperation have to date examined only the cooperation made evident by military spending.[1]

With these thoughts in mind, let us reexamine the conclusions drawn about the distribution of Western alliance military burdens and then broaden the analysis to include allied spending on Third World development assistance and research and development. This evaluation of security cooperation is broadened still further in chapter 6, as we move to a less quantitative examination of allied cooperation for purposes of international monetary management.

The analysis in this chapter is founded upon the realization that a variety of policy instruments enhance national and collective security. The security contributions made with each instrument must be examined to obtain a complete picture of the distribution of burdens among the allies. Moreover, as one relaxes the assumptions of the simple public goods model, formulates theoretical constructs that more closely approximate reality, and tests them empirically, the simplifications of earlier models tend to confuse more than they clarify. This was shown in chapter 3 when accounting for multiple goods, differences in national costs of production, the effects of political comparative advantage, and consultation among allies.

If we recognize that each alliance nation has its own preferred national security strategies and must confront political constraints—in addition to economic constraints—in their security production functions, we can then focus on the way these divergent preferences can serve common goals rather than detract from them. The findings of this chapter and the next validate the propositions put forth in chapters 3 and 4.

Externalities in Nonmilitary Security Goods

Each of the security contributions discussed in this and the next chapter produce an externality that enhances alliance security. In other words, from each contribution category a public good is produced that is consumed by all alliance nations. This is not to say that these are pure public goods—they are not. Rather, they exhibit varying degrees of publicness similar to the types of goods discussed by Bruce Russett (1970), Todd Sandler (1977), and others. The production of almost any security contribution produces privately consumable benefits for the producer aside from the externality that is consumed by all alliance nations. Jointly produced goods tend to decrease the tendency toward suboptimal provision of these public goods because of the private benefits that accrue to their producers. Instead of being able to free ride on the production of another nation, each nation can obtain only certain goods from national production and will, accordingly, produce joint products in the process. These implications combined with the possibilities of trade in public goods point to the probability of greater efficiency in alliance goods provision.

For the purposes of the following analysis, a number of ideas regarding the publicness of military goods should be reiterated. First, military forces can exhibit thinning, that is, they can be consumed at a higher level by the nation where those forces are deployed (Sandler and Cauley, 1975). Thinning results from limits to force mobility and to speed of redeployment, including limits caused by geographical barriers and distance. Thinning is manifested in the European theater to the degree that NATO's forces on the southern, central, and northern fronts cannot supplement each other when speedy reinforcement is required. American and allied overseas bases ease these effects of thinning. Second, alliance defense expenditures produce benefits that are private between nations but public within nations; in other words, these expenditures yield joint products that have public and private components. Examples of the private benefits are military forces that can be used to maintain internal order or to deter an individual adversary (e.g., Greek and Turkish forces as they deter each other). Nonetheless, a significant component of these expenditures help achieve collective goals.

Development assistance spending also yields both private and public benefits. First, foreign aid to an underdeveloped country promotes that country's political stability and reliability. Western donations contribute to the political orientation of the recipient, thus enhancing Western security in the developed world. Abraham Lowenthal (1987) has argued that development aid to Latin American was motivated almost purely by Western security concerns rather than by the benevolence of Western donor nations. Second, foreign aid contributes economically to the security of commercial activities for all Western nations involved in the recipient's economy by promoting economic growth and stability; this, in turn, promotes lower-risk investments and higher returns. Additionally, a stable Third World economy also helps the allies ensure against outside intervention in these countries. Last, and specifically relevant to the United States, the United States likely receives public spillovers from the aid donations made by other allies because of the negative sentiment toward American hegemony. The United States is thus able to look as if it is not involved in this area of Western affairs while consuming the pro-Western orientations cultivated by allied spending.

One also needs to account for the concessional nature of foreign aid donations; concessional financial flows are aid donations with an outright grant component. Concessional flows include aid given with no conditions of repayment and loans that are made at below market rates. The higher the portion of concessional components in a donor's aid package, the larger the public component. Official development assistance to developing countries thus yields fewer private benefits to the donor. Nonconcessional loans, obviously, yield a backpay that is not associated with concessional aid and thus engender higher private benefits.[2]

The limits of the publicness of foreign aid appear when the goals and objectives of one alliance nation diverge from the goals and objectives of Western nations generally. Where goals and objectives do not converge, the benefits the donor receives from foreign aid are private. The various stands taken over the years by Western allies regarding the Arab-Israeli conflict illustrate how allied foreign policy goals diverge. Intra-alliance differences on the conflicts in Indochina in the postwar period are also cases in point.

In 1989 NATO publicly renewed its commitment to cooperation on the alliance's "third dimension." Research and development programs and their findings can be classified as pure public goods, since they are not limited to consumption by the Western club. Military technological advances are public goods, but only for the West. Technology sharing within the alliance can also be viewed as private good payments for increased public goods production (discussed in chapter 3 and the alternative public goods model in appendix B). In other words, technology developed in a country consuming a public good produced by another alliance country can be shared by the former country as payment for the public spillover from the latter. So even where private goods exist within the alliance context, they still may be relevant to alliance trades and security cooperation.

Although they are not directly related to research and development spending, the activities of the Coordinating Committee (COCOM) for multilateral export controls must be taken into account. COCOM activities produce a public good for the Western club by limiting technology transfer to adversary economies. In the early 1990s it began to reevaluate its restricted commodities list and its list of "proscribed destination" countries to account for the changing security problems in the international environment. In particular, COCOM liberalized its technology control policies as they applied to former Soviet bloc economies and member countries of the former Soviet Union, orienting controls more toward the threat of weapons proliferation in the Third World (Wendt, 1990; Auerbach, 1990).

The Bretton Woods international economic system sought to provide stability and predictability to the international economy following World War II. Until 1971, these efforts—and since then cooperative economic management—produced the public goods of economic stability and predictability or, more broadly, maintained the liberal economic order. To the extent that stability and predictability are consumable by all nations, stabilization efforts are a pure public good. But efforts in the 1980s toward monetary stabilization were aimed almost exclusively at solving the economic problems of Western nations and thus generally excluded others from consumption.[3]

Private goods (and thus mixed goods, or joint products) are also integral to the goods trading system in the alliance (see appendix B). Private goods, such as access to another nation's market in international trade or inward flows of investment to a nation to help finance a budget deficit, can be viewed as payment by one country to another for increased public goods production. In this way, two types of goods are traded among alliance members, as laid out in the second alternative public goods model (appendix B). Thus both private and public goods are traded among alliance members, and both are important in evaluating the efficiency and equity of alliance security burden sharing.

What follows in this chapter and the next is an aggregate analysis of security contributions in four alliance contribution categories: defense spending, foreign aid, research and development, and monetary stabilization.[4]

Methodological Choice

In any research, methodological choices must be made. These choices are particularly important when one challenges conventional wisdom because of the need to clarify the interpretation of empirical findings of earlier studies. At times, however, these choices tend to confuse the reader; indeed, confusion is the state of the art in studies of alliance burden sharing. For instance, a great deal of evidence—mostly in the work of Todd Sandler and his associates—suggests that the validity of the free-rider hypothesis declined during the postwar era. There is also evidence (mostly in Oneal's work) that the alliance is still a "uniquely privileged group" that continues to exhibit strong free-rider tendencies. And there is evidence on both sides of the Nash-Lindahl behavior assumptions: Glenn Palmer (1989) found evidence of Lindahl (cooperative) behavior, while others found support for the Nash (noncooperative) assumption. At least some of these contradictions can be blamed on differing methodological approaches. In addition, sophisticated multivariate regression techniques are the modal choice for analyses of burden sharing. The following examination of quantitative indicators of burden sharing takes a different and simpler approach.

First, one goal is to reexamine the original Olson and Zeckhauser model and its findings to determine whether or not they hold for other expenditure categories and for later postwar years. In that work, simple rank-order correlations tested the degree to which economic size correlated with the military burdens borne by alliance members. Olson and Zeckhauser found that there was a positive correlation between size and military spending and took this as support for the hypothesis that the small exploit the large in the Western alliance. Thus, the first task of any study challenging those findings should be to reproduce the Olson and Zeckhauser findings and determine whether they are replicable across both time and alliance contribution categories. Accordingly, rank-order correlations are produced for allied spending on the military, on development assistance, and on research and development for 1960–87.[5]

Second, the multiple security contribution framework developed earlier presents an unusual problem for the analyst evaluating the distribution of Western alliance security burdens in that it does not allow identification of a single dependent variable or a causal relationship between that dependent variable and a number of independent variables. Given that the ideas presented in chapter 3 point to the trade-offs among alliance security categories, it is more appropriate to term the categories *interdependent* variables rather than *dependent or independent* variables. To move past this problem, one could build a simultaneous equations model to test the framework across contribution categories, but the analyst does not receive enough theoretical guidance in the existing literature to identify the configuration of the independent variables. Therefore, at this stage in the theoretical development of the multiple public goods framework, it seems prudent to choose a straightforward methodology, free from the restrictive assumptions of most multivariate statistical techniques.

Nonetheless, after examining the aggregate analysis of the strength of allied free riding as shown by the correlation results, I was left with only a partial picture of allied burden sharing. I was also interested in generating evaluations of the individual efforts of the allied nations. This is where regression techniques have their strength, as they are able to disaggregate results better than correlation analysis. But as mentioned above, the theoretical models are insufficient at present to produce such analysis. Consequently, the second portion of analysis in this chapter examines the relative percentages of gross domestic product devoted to the three types of contributions in order to evaluate the particular national burdens of alliance security. While not a sophisticated methodological approach, this exposition of relative expenditures allows the reader to examine the security efforts made by allied nations. In this way, I hope to reveal national priorities in each area and test the specialization hypothesis discussed above.

Of course, a more appropriate way to analyze a variety of security expenditures might be to sum these expenditures for a given year for a given alliance nation and take the total outlay as the total burden. This approach was taken by John Oneal (1990b) in his work on military expenditure and foreign aid. This approach, however, is purely input oriented and assumes that a given level of expenditure in any of two or more categories yields an equal amount of security. That is, it assumes that a dollar spent on the military yields the same amount of security as a dollar spent on development aid. This assumption is not valid and indicates the need for a disaggregated analysis of expenditure categories.[6]

Contributions, Shifting Burdens, and Alliance Success

The first task of the correlation analysis is to reexamine Olson and Zeckhauser's analysis of alliance military expenditures and to determine whether the empirical support they obtained for their model holds up for years other than those in their study. Specifically, the following analysis reproduces the first correlation contained in Olson and Zeckhauser's analysis and correlates total gross domestic product with the share of GDP spent on the military.[7] Moreover, in contrast to the second portion of Olson and Zeckhauser's analysis, this study does not factor out infrastructure costs from the military expenditure figures for each nation. This decision was made in order to maintain data comparability across the alliance dimensions analyzed. Only if a component comparable to infrastructure was evident for each dimension could infrastructure costs be legitimately factored out of the military dimension. Additionally, computing the correlations for 1960 using Olson and Zeckhauser's methodology (factoring out infrastructure costs) or my methodology does not yield substantially different results.[8]

Table 5.1 displays the correlations between GDP and expenditure share of GDP for the three spending categories. The results on military spending support the results of Sandler and Forbes (1980), which point to the declining strength of the small-exploit-the-large relationship among the Western allies since 1960. The strength of the correlation for 1960 was not repeated after that year and decreased substantially after 1966, indicating that the adoption of flexible response did have an impact on the distribution of alliance military burdens. This may also have resulted from increased intra-European reliance resulting from the growing efforts at integration among the European Community countries (Oneal, 1990b). More important, however, this table shows that the conventional wisdom of the free-rider hypothesis has little grounding.

Not surprisingly, considering the small percentage of gross domestic product Japan spends on the military, adding Japan and Spain to the military correlation series yields even weaker results. (They were even negative for six years, although those correlations are extremely weak.) Counting Japan as a Western alliance country has significant implications for the hypotheses of the Olson and Zeckhauser model. However, if one disaggregates the Western alliance system and analyzes military expenditures from the perspective of a bilateral U.S.-Japanese alliance and a multilateral NATO, then Japanese behavior fits with the Olson and Zeckhauser model. But to do this, one would have had to assume that alliance military security interests in the Pacific could be separated from those in the Atlantic. Considering the global nature of Western economic interests and the history of the perceived Soviet military threat, this was not a valid assumption.

Moreover, disaggregation would have required some division of

TABLE 5.1
Spearman Rank-Order Correlations between Gross Domestic Product and Share of Gross Domestic Product Devoted to Military Expenditures, Foreign Aid, and Research and Development, 1960–1987, Western Alliance Countries

Year	Military spending, including Spain and Japan[a]	Military spending, excluding Spain and Japan[b]	Foreign aid[c]	Research and development[d]
1960	.362	.455	.564	
1961	.164	.323	.464	
1962	.241	.411	.473	
1963	.268	.442	.518	
1964	.241	.411	.482	
1965	.182	.389	.418	
1966	.164	.358	.436	
1967	.126	.314	.264	.383 (9)
1968	.102	.284	.109	
1969	.044	.240	−.064	.394 (10)
1970	.044	.182	−.445	.467 (10)
1971	−.008	.116	−.364	.552 (10)
1972	.029	.165	−.464	.618 (11)
1973	.021	.156	−.545	.430 (10)
1974	.038	.182	−.564	.400 (9)
1975	−.068	.103	−.636	.479 (10)
1976	−.044	.134	−.664	.536 (11)
1977	.003	.200	−.673	.357 (8)
1978	−.012	.178	−.745	.527 (10)
1979	.032	.235	−.709	.430 (10)
1980	−.003	.191	−.673	.483 (9)
1981	−.006	.191	−.600	.482 (11)
1982	.009	.209	−.673	.533 (9)
1983	.124	.358	−.645	.588 (10)
1984	.059	.262	−.727	.714 (7)
1985	.088	.301	−.763	.048 (8)
1986	.082	.297	−.827	.486 (6)
1987	.056	.266	−.800	

[a]$N = 16$.
[b]$N = 14$.
[c]$N = 11$.
[d]N in parentheses.

American military expenditures by regional mission so as to provide values for regional comparison. The conceptual and methodological problems would have ranged from multiple missions for particular forces to the influence of regional security on Western interests. The military problems in the Persian Gulf and their impact on the interests of all Western nations are perfect examples of this conceptual problem. These division problems have been thoroughly discussed in Alice Maroni and John Ulrich (1985).

The Olson and Zeckhauser correlations for foreign aid expenditures of developed nations were .770 for 1960 and .439 for 1962, using two data sets. They concluded that "there is some tendency toward disproportionate burden sharing, but that private, or purely national, benefits from foreign aid are probably also very important" (1966:276). These results are in stark contrast to the correlations of later years shown in table 5.1. The table shows that, while moderate correlations were obtained for the early years, strong negative relationships were obtained for the later years. Although the trend began slightly before 1973, the strength of the negative correlation increased after the first oil crisis.

The data thus suggest that small alliance nations bear disproportionate alliance foreign aid burdens. Quite possibly, the oil crisis sensitized these small nations to their energy vulnerability, thus prodding them to increase donations to energy-relevant countries. (Energy-relevant countries include not only energy producers but also those located at strategically important locations, such as those surrounding sea-lanes.) Moreover, the largest alliance nation, the United States, has always been less resource dependent and thus may not have reacted in the same manner as the small countries. Only analysis of bilateral aid flow data could yield verification of this possible cause. Even so, the results suggest that the distribution of allied burdens across dimensions does not follow a consistent pattern. In other words, different nations devote different amounts of resources to different policy instruments.

The research and development correlations show the greatest apparent support for Olson and Zeckhauser's model. In general, these correlations are stronger than Olson and Zeckhauser's military correlations. But this result should not be surprising, as proportional research and development expenditures are likely to parallel gross domestic product, since small nations are likely to devote relatively greater economic resources to maintaining their economic welfare, while larger nations have a greater surplus of resources available for research and development. In other words, the free-rider hypothesis might manifest itself on the research and development dimension, because small nations have access to the public good of an alliance knowledge base and, therefore, do not have as great a need for technological innovation. Large economies have greater demand for innovation and more opportunities to generate such innovation.

The free-rider hypothesis, therefore, does not hold up across dimensions. Support for the hypothesis on the military dimension, the dimension for which it has received the most political and intellectual attention, has broken down since the original analysis, which used data for 1960 and 1964. Only the research and development dimension shows the strong positive correlations hypothesized by the Olson and Zeckhauser model. But beyond uncovering what the overall relationship is between gross domestic product and its shares in the three spending categories—thus testing the free-rider hypothesis—correlation analysis provides little insight into the actual distribution of alliance burdens among the alliance nations and the degree to which specialization of contributions occurs across those dimensions. Only by examining the gross domestic product shares on each of these three dimensions can we know the distribution of burdens and the specialization tendencies.

The military data for sixteen alliance countries is displayed in table 5.2, which shows a wide range of share values among alliance countries. In general, the United States, the United Kingdom, Turkey, Greece, and Portugal (in earlier years) show the highest percentage of gross domestic product devoted to military expenditure, while Japan, Spain, Luxembourg, and in the middle years, Canada show the lowest percentages. American military expenditures remained one of the highest, if not the highest, of all alliance nations throughout this time period. Even during the post-Vietnam demobilization (dubbed the "decade of neglect" by the Reagan administration), the American military share was surpassed only by Greece, Turkey, and Portugal in various years. In light of the relatively high historic public support for military spending in the United States, this is an area where an alliance nation has put its political comparative advantage to good use. Portugal's expenditures declined in the mid-1970s in response to Portuguese decolonization and are in midrange (seventh out of sixteen) of alliance military shares in 1987. Turkish and Greek shares were also high, likely in response to the recurring conflict in the 1970s between the two nations over the island of Cyprus. The Turkish expenditure share peaked in the mid-1970s, while the Greek share remained high into the 1980s. But regardless of the reasons for these expenditures, their forces remained part of alliance military forces, enhancing military security, and can be seen as disproportionate alliance military burdens.

TABLE 5.2
Portion of Alliance Countries' Gross Domestic Product Devoted to
Military Spending, 1960–1987

Year	BE	CA	DE	FR	WG	GR	IT	LU
1960	3.63	4.27	2.70	6.46	4.00	4.86	3.06	1.01
1961	3.48	4.22	2.58	6.31	3.97	4.24	2.90	1.11
1962	3.53	4.10	3.01	6.14	4.78	4.05	2.97	1.29
1963	3.46	3.61	3.01	5.64	5.21	3.83	3.10	1.19
1964	3.44	3.50	2.82	5.41	4.65	3.57	3.07	1.38
1965	3.21	2.90	2.81	5.23	4.34	3.50	3.10	1.36
1966	3.16	2.76	2.69	5.11	4.15	3.58	3.17	1.35
1967	3.24	2.86	2.65	5.11	4.33	4.35	2.91	1.11
1968	3.16	2.57	2.75	4.92	3.62	4.69	2.77	0.92
1969	2.98	2.30	2.46	4.38	3.61	4.79	2.53	0.83
1970	2.96	2.33	2.32	4.18	3.34	4.75	2.48	0.76
1971	2.87	2.21	2.44	4.00	3.39	4.69	2.70	0.79
1972	2.86	2.08	2.25	3.87	3.49	4.56	2.88	0.82
1973	2.79	1.90	2.04	3.80	3.48	4.10	2.67	0.78
1974	2.79	1.90	2.29	3.75	3.62	4.28	2.58	0.76
1975	3.08	1.84	2.44	3.85	3.66	6.53	2.48	0.97
1976	3.16	1.83	2.27	3.81	3.47	6.91	2.30	0.99
1977	3.22	1.91	2.28	3.91	3.35	7.03	2.38	1.01
1978	3.34	1.95	2.34	3.98	3.35	6.70	2.39	1.03
1979	3.34	1.76	2.32	3.95	3.26	6.28	2.39	1.02
1980	3.36	1.79	2.44	4.03	3.28	5.67	2.42	1.15
1981	3.53	1.78	2.53	4.17	3.39	6.98	2.46	1.21
1982	3.41	2.06	2.51	4.15	3.39	6.91	2.61	1.18
1983	3.33	2.01	2.45	4.19	3.37	6.33	2.67	1.18
1984	3.22	2.12	2.33	4.12	3.26	7.21	2.67	1.12
1985	3.07	2.16	2.18	4.07	3.19	7.11	2.71	1.07
1986	3.05	2.16	2.01	3.90	3.11	6.18	2.24	1.10
1987	3.00	2.11	2.12	3.95	3.06	6.28	2.43	1.21

Source: Based on OECD (1987); SIPRI (various years).
Note: Values are given as percentages.

As for nations on the lower end of the military spectrum, Japan is the most notable because of its economic size. Nonetheless, in addition to its 1 percent of gross domestic product defense spending ceiling (which was breached in the late 1980s), the Japanese public prefers to use other tools in pursuit of security. Denmark and Italy also show relatively low military shares, overall.

The results of this table correspond to the results of Sandler and his associates. In particular, Todd Sandler and John Forbes (1980)

NE	NW	PO	SP	TU	UK	US	J
3.89	3.20	4.23	1.95	5.13	6.44	8.84	1.03
4.29	3.27	6.40	1.78	5.46	6.22	8.99	0.91
4.33	3.53	7.02	1.90	5.15	6.30	9.15	0.96
4.21	3.51	6.45	1.80	4.72	6.11	8.66	0.95
4.13	3.43	6.70	1.74	4.82	6.00	7.92	0.92
3.77	3.75	6.21	1.68	5.00	5.84	7.39	0.91
3.56	3.57	6.28	1.82	4.40	5.64	8.27	0.88
3.72	3.51	7.27	1.86	4.54	5.64	9.28	0.84
3.44	3.61	7.34	1.80	4.60	5.33	9.09	0.80
3.41	3.60	6.74	1.68	4.33	4.92	8.49	0.78
3.27	3.47	7.05	1.63	4.29	4.76	7.71	0.78
3.27	3.39	7.38	1.61	4.54	4.88	6.83	0.83
3.22	3.29	6.92	1.61	4.30	5.10	6.45	0.85
3.10	3.13	5.93	1.62	4.14	4.77	5.83	0.82
3.13	3.04	7.40	1.66	3.86	4.96	5.90	0.87
3.29	3.21	5.28	1.71	6.07	4.88	5.74	0.91
3.04	3.12	4.02	1.76	6.13	4.85	5.16	0.90
3.31	3.10	3.53	1.73	5.77	4.68	5.13	0.90
3.08	3.22	3.47	1.68	5.19	4.54	4.92	0.91
3.20	3.08	3.46	1.75	4.32	4.60	4.96	0.91
3.11	2.89	3.46	1.89	4.29	5.01	5.36	0.92
3.20	2.89	3.54	1.98	4.88	4.79	5.65	0.93
3.23	3.02	3.45	2.23	5.19	5.03	6.29	0.94
3.19	3.08	3.37	2.41	4.83	5.32	6.48	0.97
3.20	2.80	3.28	2.47	4.41	5.03	6.38	0.97
3.11	3.10	3.16	2.43	4.49	5.18	6.69	0.98
3.06	3.12	3.17	2.00	4.75	4.90	6.76	1.00
3.07	3.32	3.08	2.08	4.25	4.59	6.44	1.01

Abbreviations: BE, Belgium; *CA*, Canada; *DE*, Denmark; *FR*, France; *WG*, West Germany; *GR*, Greece; *IT*, Italy; *LU*, Luxembourg; *NE*, The Netherlands; *NW*, Norway; *PO*, Poland; *SP*, Spain; *TU*, Turkey; *UK*, United Kingdom; *US*, United States; *J*, Japan.

found that Italy and Canada were free riding in the defense realm, which roughly corresponds with my results. James Murdoch and Sandler (1982) saw West Germany, the United Kingdom, Canada, and Turkey as free riders, although the military shares I show for Turkey do not support their conclusion. The results for the United Kingdom and Germany are somewhat different from those of Sandler and his associates but, nonetheless, show that even large nations do not devote a high percentage of their gross domestic product to the military.

TABLE 5.3
**Portion of Alliance Countries' Gross Domestic Product Devoted to
Official Development Assistance, 1960–1987**

Year	BE	CA	DE	FR	WG
1960	0.91	0.19	0.08	1.41	0.33
1961	0.78	0.15	0.12	1.44	0.40
1962	0.55	0.08	0.11	1.33	0.44
1963	0.59	0.15	0.11	1.00	0.41
1964	0.47	0.16	0.11	0.91	0.44
1965	0.61	0.18	0.13	0.76	0.40
1966	0.43	0.32	0.19	0.70	0.34
1967	0.47	0.31	0.21	0.72	0.41
1968	0.43	0.25	0.23	0.69	0.42
1969	0.51	0.32	0.38	0.71	0.38
1970	0.47	0.41	0.37	0.66	0.28
1971	0.52	0.41	0.42	0.68	0.34
1972	0.55	0.45	0.44	0.68	0.31
1973	0.52	0.41	0.46	0.58	0.32
1974	0.51	0.46	0.53	0.61	0.38
1975	0.61	0.53	0.54	0.62	0.40
1976	0.51	0.45	0.51	0.61	0.36
1977	0.48	0.49	0.55	0.59	0.33
1978	0.57	0.50	0.69	0.57	0.37
1979	0.59	0.45	0.70	0.60	0.45
1980	0.51	0.40	0.73	0.64	0.44
1981	0.60	0.40	0.70	0.73	0.47
1982	0.59	0.40	0.74	0.74	0.48
1983	0.59	0.44	0.71	0.74	0.48
1984	0.58	0.48	0.83	0.77	0.45
1985	0.55	0.47	0.76	0.78	0.47
1986	0.49	0.47	0.85	0.70	0.43
1987	0.49	0.46	0.85	0.74	0.39

Source: Based on OECD (1987); OECD (various years).
Notes: Ideally, this table would include foreign aid data for all Western alliance
countries, but cross-national comparable data is available only for the eleven nations
shown here.

The overseas development assistance shares shown in table 5.3
show a somewhat different picture of the distribution of alliance burdens.[9] The most striking figures show that, in contrast to the role as
mainstay of alliance military defense, the United States is at the low
end of alliance aid giving, rivaled only by Italy and Japan, and to a
lesser degree, the United Kingdom. Italy later increased its aid giving
(its continued ability to do so may be affected by public opinion, as

IT	NE	NW	UK	US	J
0.24	0.30	0.11	0.56	0.53	0.24
0.19	0.44	0.14	0.59	0.55	0.20
0.21	0.47	0.12	0.52	0.56	0.14
0.13	0.25	0.17	0.48	0.59	0.20
0.08	0.28	0.16	0.53	0.56	0.14
0.10	0.35	0.16	0.47	0.49	0.27
0.12	0.43	0.18	0.45	0.44	0.27
0.21	0.48	0.18	0.43	0.43	0.31
0.18	0.47	0.30	0.40	0.37	0.24
0.15	0.48	0.31	0.38	0.32	0.25
0.13	0.57	0.33	0.32	0.28	0.20
0.17	0.55	0.33	0.40	0.30	0.22
0.08	0.64	0.42	0.38	0.28	0.20
0.12	0.51	0.45	0.33	0.22	0.24
0.13	0.59	0.56	0.40	0.25	0.24
0.09	0.70	0.65	0.39	0.26	0.23
0.12	0.76	0.70	0.39	0.25	0.19
0.09	0.81	0.82	0.44	0.24	0.21
0.14	0.78	0.87	0.46	0.26	0.23
0.08	0.93	0.91	0.52	0.19	0.27
0.17	0.96	0.84	0.35	0.27	0.32
0.19	1.07	0.82	0.43	0.19	0.27
0.23	1.07	1.00	0.37	0.26	0.28
0.23	0.90	1.06	0.33	0.24	0.32
0.32	1.02	0.97	0.34	0.23	0.34
0.31	0.91	0.99	0.34	0.24	0.29
0.40	0.99	1.15	0.31	0.23	0.29
0.35	0.98	1.07	0.27	0.20	0.31

Values are given as percentages.
Abbreviations: BE, Belgium; *CA*, Canada; *DE*, Denmark; *FR*, France; *WG*, West Germany; *IT*, Italy; *NE*, The Netherlands; *NW*, Norway; *UK*, United Kingdom; *US*, United States; *J*, Japan.

shown in chapter 4). Japan's aid donations will likely increase in the 1990s because of government pledges and its past success in meeting its aid pledges (Bobrow and Boyer, 1985:1–2). In fact, in 1989 Japan surpassed the United States as the world's largest foreign aid donor in absolute terms.

This development is part of a pattern that has seen Japan's share of total Western foreign aid donations rise from 9 percent in 1980 to 32 percent by 1987 (Starrels, 1989). Additionally, one Liberal Democratic party official stated that, although the annual growth in military expenditure would decline, the 7 percent annual growth rate for overseas development assistance would continue.[10] In other words, Japan appeared to be giving in to allied pressure (applied especially at the annual Western economic summits) to assume economic burdens commensurate with its economic strength. In addition, both Japan and Italy appear to do more in the foreign aid realm when noncongressional publicly funded loans are included in the foreign aid figures (Boyer 1990:254). Including private flows in the Japanese figures pushes them upward. It also indicates, however, that both countries (and particularly Japan) have taken a more profit-minded approach to foreign aid donations than is the case for other nations. Japanese loans to Third World countries, however, will likely decrease (at least in a relative sense) as Japan expands the geographical scope of its aid donations outside of Asia and into areas where loan repayment is precluded on grounds of financial exigency.

At the high end of foreign aid burdens, France, Denmark, Norway, and the Netherlands have borne larger aid burdens than other alliance nations. This supports the assertion made by Stanley Sloan (1985a, 1985b) that the Europeans prefer nonmilitary approaches to security, particularly when dealing with alliance-relevant problems in the Third World. This may be related to the Lomé conventions that helped solidify preferential economic relationships and increased aid flows between members of the European Community and forty-six Atlantic-Caribbean-Pacific countries.

The foreign aid findings are especially relevant when we consider that Norway and Denmark were not at the higher end of the military share distribution, indicating specialization in contributions. The primary bearers of military burdens were Turkey, Greece, the United States, at times Portugal, and to a lesser extent the United Kingdom. On the military dimension, France was on the high end in the early 1960s but dropped to the middle range of share values, at least partially due to its severing of colonial ties. The Netherlands and Norway were in the midrange throughout the 1960–85 period; and Denmark was somewhat below the midrange. We could even call the United States a free rider on the foreign aid dimension. Accordingly, taking the military and foreign aid data together supports the specialization hypothesis.

A third distribution of alliance security burdens is evident in table 5.4, listing the research and development shares of Western alliance countries. The United States registers the highest shares, with France, the United Kingdom, West Germany, and the Netherlands not far

TABLE 5.4
Portion of Alliance Countries' Gross Domestic Product Devoted to Research and Development, 1967–1986

Year	CA	DE	FR	WG	IT	NE	NW	PO	SP	UK	US	J
1967	0.87	0.46	1.00	0.86	0.10	0.87	0.66		0.13	1.22		
1969	0.94		1.27	0.77	0.36	0.87	0.67		0.10	1.20	1.57	0.48
1970	0.80	0.50	1.14	0.93	0.38	0.89	0.64	0.25	0.11		1.62	0.50
1971	0.86		1.12	1.02	0.37	0.92	0.73		0.15	1.00	1.37	0.55
1972	0.81		1.08	1.09	0.38	0.92	0.79	0.24	0.15		1.45	0.56
1973	0.74	0.51	1.01	1.04	0.40	0.86	0.78		0.14		1.34	0.56
1974	0.70		1.01	1.07	0.34	0.84	0.77		0.12	1.04	1.27	0.58
1975	0.70		0.98	1.06	0.40	0.91	0.80		0.15		1.27	0.60
1976	0.66	0.56	0.92	1.01	0.39	0.90	0.84	0.20	0.14		1.24	0.59
1977	0.67		0.91	0.95	0.42	0.89	0.86				1.22	0.58
1978	0.66			1.01	0.41	0.89	0.87	0.25	0.17	0.98	1.18	0.60
1979	0.61	0.52	0.92	1.02	0.37	0.90	0.81		0.19		1.19	0.61
1980	0.62		0.95		0.39	0.90	0.75	0.17	0.20		1.19	0.61
1981	0.63	0.57	1.07	1.04	0.48	0.89	0.74		0.21	1.12	1.21	0.63
1982	0.69		1.16	1.09	0.51	0.96	0.73	0.22			1.28	0.62
1983	0.71	0.58	1.18	1.05	0.33	0.96			0.22	1.07	1.30	0.61
1984	0.73		1.25			0.93	0.73	0.24	0.22		1.30	
1985	0.69	0.58		0.99	0.69	0.93	0.74		0.24			0.59
1986					0.63	0.98		0.23		0.89	1.32	0.59

Sources: Based on OECD (1987, 1984, 1985); UNESCO (various years).
Note: Values are given as percentages.
Abbreviations: CA, Canada; DE, Denmark; FR, France; WG, West Germany; IT, Italy; NE, The Netherlands; NW, Norway; PO, Poland; SP, Spain; UK, United Kingdom; US, United States; J, Japan.

behind. One would expect these industrialized economies to be leaders in science and technology efforts; one would also expect alliance cooperation on this third dimension to take the form of technological assistance flowing from these economies to others in the alliance. It would be instructive to examine more closely the activities of COCOM to understand exactly what R&D intensive economies do with their output and, also, what restrictions are placed on technology transfer outside the members of COCOM.

A surprising finding in table 5.4 is that Japan does not register a higher share of R&D. This may be because of close cooperation between the public and private sectors in the Japanese economy, making public R&D funding unimportant in government security expenditures.[11] A closer examination of Japanese R&D spending for 1986, for example, bears this point out: UNESCO figures show that 79 percent of Japanese spending is funded from the private sector, with only 21 percent coming from government funds. This is contrasted with American R&D funding, wherein only 50 percent is funded by the private sector and 46 percent is funded by the government.[12] This also corresponds to the low Japanese foreign aid percentages and the use of private funds.

Considering their somewhat marginal status as developed countries, one would expect Spain and Portugal to register relatively low on this expenditure category. Italy also is at the lower end of the distribution of public R&D funding. This finding is not unusual given that Italy's per capita gross domestic product in 1960 and 1985 was the sixth and fifth lowest, respectively, of the sixteen alliance nations listed in table 5.2. Only Greece, Turkey, Portugal, Spain, and Japan (in 1960 only) registered lower scores on this measure.

The R&D correlations seem to support the Olson and Zeckhauser hypothesis, since four of the G-7 nations show high shares, with the others (Japan, Italy, and Canada) in the middle-to-lower range. Whether this dimension exhibits free riding or a tendency for the advanced economies to devote greater resources to R&D because the R&D infrastructure already exists could be determined by closer examination of government policies throughout the alliance. But while the share data on this dimension do not run counter to the Olson and Zeckhauser hypothesis, they still support the specialization hypothesis, as a number of countries that do not exhibit high shares on other dimensions do so here. Specifically, Japan shows low shares on military and foreign aid dimensions, but given its private-public sector relationship and its foreign aid spending, Japan should not be written off as a free rider here. West Germany was in the middle range on all the other dimensions but shows high marks in this area. Given the conventional wisdom regarding German and Japanese technological prowess, this specialization result is expected.

The following list shows the relative placement of the alliance countries on the three alliance dimensions:

Military Spending

- High: United States, United Kingdom, Greece, Turkey (Portugal and France in early years)
- Middle: West Germany, Belgium, Netherlands, Norway (Portugal and France in later years)
- Low: Japan, Spain, Luxembourg (Canada and Italy in later years)

Foreign Aid

- High: France, Netherlands (Norway and Denmark in later years)
- Middle: West Germany, Belgium, Canada, United Kingdom (Denmark in middle years)
- Low: United States, Japan, Italy (Norway, Denmark, and Canada in early years)

Research and Development

- High: United States, West Germany, Netherlands, France, United Kingdom
- Middle: Japan, Canada, Belgium, Norway, Denmark (Italy in later years)
- Low: Portugal, Spain (Italy in early years)

The United States consistently registers high contributions to military and R&D and low contributions to foreign aid. This means that the United States specializes in the production of military and R&D alliance goods but leaves the production of foreign aid goods to others.

Japan, it would seem, does not specialize in the production of any of the three categories. However, foreign aid spending in the late 1980s and early 1990s and Japanese private funding should be considered in tandem with public funding for research and development and aid. Additionally, as will be seen in the next chapter, Japan made significant contributions to Western monetary stability since the fall of Bretton Woods.

West Germany's specialization shows up on the R&D dimension, which along with Germany's midrange contributions to military spending and foreign aid keeps Germany from becoming a free rider. West Germany also makes nonbudgetary military contributions, such as foreign military bases on its soil. In the next chapter, German contributions to international monetary stability are shown as significant.

The Netherlands makes rather large contributions to alliance security, because of its high shares on all but the military dimension and its middle range on that dimension. This finding is especially interesting given the size of the Netherlands and given Olson and Zeckhauser's hypothesis regarding the behavior of smaller nations. French contributions closely parallel those of the Netherlands, although the French military share has been consistently higher. French military expenditures were among the highest of alliance countries during its most independent years (the DeGaulle years), which fits with the tenets of Sandler's joint product model. The United Kingdom's contributions are also notable, as it shows relatively high shares on all but the foreign aid dimension. This closely parallels American behavior, possibly an artifact of the Anglo-American "special relationship."

Last, in addition to the specialization tendencies of Greece, Turkey, and Portugal in the military realm, this list shows that Canada and Italy do not register high on any of the three dimensions. In their highest contributions these two countries reach only the middle range. Considering their status as members of the G-7 and their participation in other Western consultative bodies, these two nations can be considered the most significant Western alliance free riders as measured by these data. A thorough examination of other dimensions might well uncover specialized contributions by these two nations, so this conclusion is tentative.

Additional Measures of Alliance Contribution

Military expenditure, foreign aid, and R&D spending are not the only measures of allied security contributions; there are others, both inside and outside the military realm (see Adams and Munz, 1988; Knorr, 1985; Sloan, 1985a, 1987). One of these, international monetary policy coordination, is the subject of the next chapter. The following is an additional attempt to put the larger American military expenditures into perspective.

One measure of allied contribution that is often ignored is the way allied personnel are enlisted: for most allied countries, conscription is the basic mode of sustaining an adequate armed force. The U.S. force is volunteer. This factor is important, because a volunteer force skews the American military budget upward in comparison to European military budgets. In addition, most European conscripts serve in the military reserve after their basic tour of duty, something that may or may not occur when American volunteers complete their period of enlistment.

Additionally, the numbers of productive individuals withdrawn from European civilian sectors is also important to burden-sharing measures. Correlations of national population with the percentage of that population in the military for the years 1968–84 yield weak negative correlations. While military expenditure and gross domestic product correlate in some years, personnel-population correlations indicate that some nations with relatively low military expenditures have been pulling their weight in terms of the numbers of soldiers placed into service.

Another contribution made by non-North American allies falls into the category of host nation support. For instance, Japan provides the real estate for American bases rent free and waives taxes, custom fees, road tolls, and landing and port charges. It also contributes large labor costs ($316 million in 1988) to support American military activities in Japan. And under a new Status of U.S. Forces Agreement, by 1996 Japan will assume all utility and Japanese national labor costs tied to the American presence. West Germany has made similar contributions, and other allied nations have, as well. Other contributions that fall into this category include medical treatment and evacuation, logistical and procurement services, and maintenance and repair of base facilities (Department of Defense, 1989:70–73). The German government provides over 130,000 housing units for allied servicemen and their families. Almost 90,000 of these are free of charge. Under the U.S.-Japan Facilities Improvement Program, the Japanese provide all the housing needs for American personnel as well as large portions of support structures (like aircraft hangars) needed on American bases. All of these costs are contributions to the overseas activities of foreign forces and are thus military contributions.

Add to these contributions the quality-of-life costs borne by the non-North American allies and we obtain an even more complicated measure for burden sharing. A Eurogroup study identified these distinct costs: "Many of the European allies permit North American and Allied forces to use their training areas and to carry out exercises on private and public land. [This activity] imposes a considerable burden upon the many Europeans who have to suffer the noise, disruption, and environmental damage which results. . . . This is particularly true in the case of Germany" (Eurogroup, 1988:14). The situation is similar in Japan. For instance, 20 percent of the land on Okinawa is taken up by American military bases, creating some tension with local people interested in developing the Okinawan tourist industry. In addition, European territory has been the likely battlefield for any possible East-

West confrontation. This reality was highlighted during the early 1980s, when Reagan administration officials made a number of rather casual remarks about the chance of limited nuclear war in Europe.

Additionally, the allies have made contributions that surpass the relative weights of their economic resources and military spending (Adams and Munz, 1988:7). For instance, the European allies have provided 95 percent of the divisions, 90 percent of the manpower, 90 percent of the artillery, 80 percent of the tanks, 80 percent of the combat aircraft, and 65 percent of the major warships placed into service by NATO countries in the North Atlantic mission (Eurogroup, 1988:10). These figures further call into question the analyses of military spending that fail to account for the outputs of defense spending and the regional missions assigned to particular forces.

Last, there are economic spin-offs of alliance military security efforts. The United States often points to spending by American personnel in allied host nations to counter charges of the adverse environmental and social effects of American bases. American officials also complain of the adverse balance of payments effects caused by overseas basing, as the outflow of American dollars weakens the dollar. On the other side, however, Stanley Sloan (1985b:33) pointed out that, over the thirty-year period prior to 1985, the allies purchased much more hardware from American defense contractors than the Pentagon did from allied contractors, which produced obvious benefits for American industries, employment, and balance of payments.

In some respects, the additional pieces of the burden-sharing picture provided in this section make an evaluation of the equity of alliance security burdens more difficult. But they also counter the argument that American military burdens far outweigh that of other allies. As we saw with foreign aid and research and development spending and will see in the next chapter as well, the United States is not as clearly the benevolent provider (or the sucker for free-riding allies) when we look beyond the military realm. And even in the military realm, that picture is not quite so clear.

Conclusions

This chapter set out to test the conventional wisdom about Western alliance burden sharing over time and across three security spending categories and shows that the conventional wisdom that small nations exploit large nations is an oversimplification of the reality of alliance affairs. While the free-rider hypothesis may have had some validity early in the postwar period, it lost credence with time and also does not hold up when one examines nonmilitary security contributions. In other words, although the United States bore most of the burdens of alliance security as the allies rebuilt immediately after the war, the burdens of alliance security were later spread more evenly. This is particularly true when nonmilitary security burdens are weighed against American military predominance.

Allies specialize in the ways they contribute to alliance security. Although a nation may appear to be free riding on the security contributions of other alliance members on a particular dimension, this nation does not free ride on all dimensions. Apparent free riding should lead the researcher to examine other alliance contribution dimensions to discover where that nation is contributing. In other words, there is no free lunch for members of the Western alliance club.

The evidence of contribution specialization has significant implications for the traditional theory of alliance security provision. Security provision moves closer to optimality when alliance nations specialize in security contributions. This specialization leads one to conclude that alliance security provision is not as dismal a state as is suggested by an examination of the military dimension alone. While this is a modest empirical point, as more dimensions are studied and added to the evaluations of Western security cooperation, a more efficient alliance production may be uncovered. The specialization tendencies displayed thus far fit with the public goods models presented in chapter 3 and the appendixes to the volume.

6

International Monetary Cooperation

THE BRETTON WOODS international economic system was created in 1944 in an effort to avoid the economic chaos and retaliatory international economic policies that contributed to the Great Depression and also to the outbreak of World War II. By promoting a liberal international economic order, the Bretton Woods system aimed to eliminate the mercantilistic trade policies adopted by the industrialized nations, policies that dampened international commerce in the 1930s. A liberal trading order was to be achieved through the establishment of the International Trade Organization (ITO) and eventually emerged as the General Agreements on Tariffs and Trade (GATT). In the financial realm, the creation of the International Monetary Fund (IMF) and the International Bank for Reconstruction and Development (IBRD)—later changed to the World Bank—were to provide stability and predictability for a system desperately in need of capital in the aftermath of World War II and the subsequent rebuilding process.

Implicit in the Bretton Woods system was the desirability of stability and predictability in international finance. Bretton Woods also aimed to avoid the problem of the old gold standard through multilateralism and the continued role of the United States in world affairs (Wightman, forthcoming). Volatile international financial markets were seen as having the following detrimental effects (BIS, 1985/86: 151–52, 1987/88:175):

■ Overvalued currencies yield powerful protectionist sentiments in countries with strong currencies. Such tendencies are counter to liberal trade practices.

- Large exchange rate fluctuations give the wrong or ambiguous signals for resource allocation, especially in terms of long-term investment.
- For goods that are internationally traded, many believed that exchange rate volatility demands higher profit margins to induce future investment in those sectors.
- Exchange rate volatility complicates domestic macroeconomic planning and management, because a country's relationship with other economies is uncertain.
- Disruptive effects on domestic price stability also arise.

Under the Bretton Woods system, the problem of financial stability was largely taken care of through the establishment of a fixed (but adjustable) exchange rate system under the auspices of the IMF. Exchange rates were tied directly to the value of the dollar, and the dollar was pegged to gold. But after Bretton Woods fell in the early 1970s, the fixed exchange rate system vanished and was replaced by a flexible exchange rate system. This chapter examines cooperation under the flexible rate system, with an eye toward the contributions made by allies to international economic stablity. The central assumption is that, even though the more rigid, and therefore predictable, fixed rate system was abandoned in the early 1970s, stability, predictability, and a commitment to liberal economic practices in international economic affairs were not abandoned. This chapter focuses on the efforts made to achieve such goals after Bretton Woods, taking into account contributions to economic prosperity through efforts to maintain monetary stability. The following analysis focuses on those alliance nations that find monetary contributions an appropriate way of contributing to alliance security. These nations produce a public good for the alliance that promotes stability and predictability and generally enhances Western economic welfare.

The burden-sharing dimension in this chapter is not as conducive to quantitative analysis as the measures in chapter 5. We could examine central bank open-market operations to determine the amount of national activity in international currency markets, but without combining these quantities with policy decisions (changes in discount rates and fiscal contractions and expansions), such evidence yields an incomplete, or even misleading, picture of national policies. Moreover, an examination of central bank currency interventions also confronts limits to the availability of data on the exact currencies purchased by central banking authorities.[1] Also, the econometric techniques required to model these relationships are beyond the scope of this book.

I have, instead taken another tack. My analysis of international monetary cooperation among the Western alliance countries is based on the documentary evidence of policy changes and cooperation found in the annual reports of the Bank for International Settlements (BIS), supplemented by a variety of secondary studies. The BIS annual report breaks down international monetary policy problems and decisions by country. This practice is particularly helpful, given that this chapter focuses primarily on the problems of the dollar in international finance. My analysis looks at monetary policy only from the standpoint of the contributions that serve the alliance security policy goal of international financial stability.

The Rise and Fall of Bretton Woods

Beginning in World War II and continuing until the early 1970s, the United States was the principal promoter and supporter of the liberal international economic system and the primary international military security guarantor. American leadership was institutionalized with the creation of the Bretton Woods system in 1944. Right from the start, economic and other nonmilitary considerations were integral to alliance security strategies. The founding of the Bretton Woods system was predicated on the connection between economic conflict and war. William Clayton, an assistant secretary of state in 1945, felt (as did Cordell Hull—see chap. 1) that "most wars originate in economic causes" (Pollard, 1985:2). And even within NATO, the bastion of Western military security concerns, the goal of economic security was central to many strategic decisions in the immediate postwar era and was based upon Article II of the organization's charter (Holm-Pedersen, 1990).

From an alliance burden-sharing perspective, American leadership entailed many direct contributions to international security, such as the Marshall Plan, economic assistance to Japan, and the American military presence abroad. The United States also bore indirect costs of alliance security through its support of the creation of the European Economic Community in the late 1950s (such as promotion of an organization that would become a future competitor) and its acceptance of discriminatory trade barriers in Europe and Japan. But to say that the United States assumed undue burdens on behalf of the allies ignores the enormous benefits and privileges obtained by the United States through its central role. American economic prosperity during the 1950s was manifest, as rebuilding nations relied upon the American productive machinery to produce the capital and consumer goods needed in their war-torn economies and American consumers gained through access to the new goods marketed in the United States. The United States also became the Western leader in decisionmaking and strategic planning (and relished the role), to the chagrin of some of Europe's traditional world leaders. This leadership role seemed natural to Americans, given the strength and size of both the American military arsenal and the American economy.

Moreover, once it was recognized that the Bretton Woods system, and in particular the International Monetary Fund, did not possess adequate resources to fund the liquidity needs of a reconstructing world economy, the United States filled the void—albeit unintentionally—by running a balance of payments deficit, providing the needed financial fuel for recovery abroad (Ilgen, 1985:12–13). So although these policies appear rather burdensome for the United States, the promotion of a liberal economic order and decolonization created many opportunities for the United States and American entrepreneurs, because of American technological prowess and industrial expertise (Russett, 1985:218). In addition, a worldwide American presence in the immediate postwar period laid the groundwork for the internationalization of American political and economic values, which continue to serve American and Western security concerns (see Nau, 1990; Ikenberry and Kupchan, 1990).

During the 1960s, however, many of the forces behind the rapid recovery and growth in the West began to be seen as the roots of problems for the international economic system (Wightman, forthcoming). Even though the American balance of payments deficit was critical to recovery during the 1950s, its persistence into the 1960s became a point of contention among the allies. DeGaulle's open criticism of the American "exorbitant privilege" and the concern of many others over the implications of the "Triffin paradox" led to serious questions about the value and convertibility of the dollar and, more generally, about the stability of the international monetary system and the ability of the United States to continue to play the role of international banker by itself.[2] In fact, David Calleo suggested that American balance of payments problems in the 1960s were a form of American-imposed burden sharing on the rest of the alliance (1982:101). The United States exported inflation after 1965 by running a balance of payments deficit while not devaluing its currency, thus forcing others to bear costs for American global commitments. From the American perspective, the unwillingness of the major allies to adjust their currency rates to a fixed American value was more and more perceived as costing American producers their competitiveness in international markets. This perception was held even though the deficit was largely a result of excessive domestic inflation. As Robert

Kudrle and Davis Bobrow (1991:150) asserted, the eventual break-down of the system in 1971 illustrates the "increasing influence of the allies and the decreased willingness of the United States to bear singular burdens."

It became clear during the 1960s that allied perceptions of security began to change and also diverge from one another, as the Europeans and Japan became increasingly concerned with the macroeconomic policies of the United States. This divergence set the stage for specialization in security provision. American international economic imbalances did not produce a breakdown of the system in the 1960s and were dealt with through such quick fixes as the establishment of a two-tiered gold market, the Kennedy Round in GATT, and the creation of special drawing rights in the IMF to provide added liquidity for the system without supplanting the dollar's centrality in the system.

Ultimately, though, the combined and interrelated pressures of American military commitments in Vietnam, domestic policy expansion under the Great Society programs, the payments deficit, declining American commercial competitiveness, and the American refusal to actively defend the dollar made it difficult for American policymakers to sustain the dollar's role in the system. On 15 August 1971, President Nixon announced that the United States was suspending dollar-gold convertibility, devaluing the dollar on international markets and imposing an import surcharge on foreign goods. These unilateral actions took the allies by surprise and effectively ended the Bretton Woods system. A number of attempts, such as the December 1971 Smithsonian Agreement, were made to reinstitute the fixed exchange rate system, but by 1973 it was recognized that fixed rates had ended and a period of floating currencies had been ushered into the world economy.

This brief account of Western monetary affairs in the earlier post-war period, however, says little about the distribution of costs and benefits among the Western allies in this policy arena. The allies certainly benefited from American financing of reconstruction, from access to capital and liquidity through the American payments deficit, and from American guarantees of military security. It was not until the American balance of payments deficit became a "problem" and dollars glutted the market that the allies began to feel the "burdens" of the centrality of the dollar and to question the value of the dollar under the fixed-rate system (Solomon, 1982:27–28).[3] The allies began complaining about the deficit and its ability to export American inflation outside the North American continent.

Although the United States influenced Western affairs during this period, economic recovery policies were detrimental to the potential of the United States to compete economically with the allies. In many respects, the success of U.S. de facto policies led to a series of circumstances that forced it to acknowledge that it could no longer be the guarantor of all aspects of alliance security and would have to pass on the burdens and decisions of alliance security to others. We now turn to the evolution of security cooperation among the allies in the post–Bretton Woods era.

More Ado about the Dollar

The burdens of adjustment[4] in international payments in the immediate post–Bretton Woods period took on a pattern quite different from the burdens of participating in a more rigid fixed-rate system. Where under Bretton Woods the allies were limited in their abilities to influence international finance, they were now required to actively intervene in the system to maintain economic stability and desirable financial circumstances. The allies moved from recipients of dollar effects to players that could directly influence the value of the dollar on international markets. Not that the alliance was of one thought on the requirements of market activity; rather, through much of the 1970s they were committed to market adjustment rather than to financial stability and predictability.

As the Bank for International Settlements asserted in its 1976–77 annual report, the United States and Canada were committed to intervention by financial authorities to smooth out market conditions but did little to change the long-term tendencies of Western finance. In contrast, the other Group of Ten countries pursued intervention policies aimed at bringing about substantial changes in official reserves and borrowing (BIS, 1976–77:129).[5] The United States was largely content to let the market run its course during the initial period of floating. The allies, confronted with this American political and macroeconomic stance, were forced to take a larger role in promoting stability, if they wanted it. This laissez-faire American attitude contributed to the rationale for the EMS (European monetary system).

Nonetheless, the United States was not completely unresponsive to the desires of its allies, nor were the burdens of adjustment and stability immediately and gladly assumed by the allies. This new era of international finance was one of fits and starts, as allied cooperation did not live up to its potential until the mid-1980s. Table 6.1 presents a chronology of major cooperative undertakings by the allies. The following analysis is based on this chronology and fills in the table's analytic and explanatory gaps.

TABLE 6.1
Chronology of Alliance Monetary Cooperation, 1971–1987

Date	Alliance nations	Action taken
December 1971	Group of Ten	Smithsonian Agreement
June–July 1972	European countries and Japan	Purchase of dollars to maintain exchange rates
July 1973	United States, West Germany	Intervention to push dollar up (also in late 1973 and early 1974)
February 1975	United States, West Germany, Switzerland	Intervention to push dollar up and agreement on more concerted intervention to maintain market order
November 1975	United States, West Germany, United Kingdom, Italy, France, Japan	Rambouillet Summit: pledge to ensure orderly markets and stable exchange rates
June 1976	United States, West Germany, United Kingdom, Italy, France, Japan, Canada	Puerto Rico Summit: regularization of Western summit process
May 1977	United States, West Germany, United Kingdom, Italy, France, Japan, Canada	London Summit: stimulus to Tokyo Round progress in GATT
June 1977	OECD countries	Announcements leading to fall of dollar
June 1977–May 1978	Japan, West Germany	Intervention to stabilize dollar
February 1978	Japan, West Germany, United States, Switzerland	Substantial interventions to strengthen dollar
April–May 1978	Japan, West Germany, United States	Further action to strengthen dollar (action successful)
July 1978	United States, West Germany, United Kingdom, Italy, France, Japan, Canada	Bonn Summit: French President Giscard d'Estaing's proclamation of "a new era of mutual trust among the seven"
October–November 1978	United States, Switzerland	Action to stabilize dollar

TABLE 6.1
Continued

Date	Alliance nations	Action taken
November 1978	West Germany, United States, Japan, Switzerland	Large-scale intervention announced; increased swap lines among the four; other actions by United States to strengthen dollar; evidence of U.S. commitment to market intervention
March–April 1979	Japan, West Germany, Switzerland	Intervention to halt rapid depreciation of their currencies relative to dollar
June 1979	United States, West Germany, United Kingdom, Italy, France, Japan, Canada	Tokyo Summit: dominance of energy issues
1980	Japan, West Germany, Switzerland	Relaxation of restrictions on capital inflows to ease demand for their currencies
June 1980	United States, West Germany, United Kingdom, Italy, France, Japan, Canada	Venice Summit: institutionalization of summits
1981	United States	Institution of tight money and anti-inflationary policies by Federal Reserve Bank and Reagan administration; ascension of dollar into 1980s heights
April 1981	United States	U.S. Treasury Secretary Regan's announcement to not regularly intervene in foreign exchange markets
July 1981	United States, West Germany, United Kingdom, Italy, France, Japan, Canada	Ottawa Summit: a "nondecisional" summit

TABLE 6.1
Continued

Date	Alliance nations	Action taken
June 1982	United States, West Germany, United Kingdom, Italy, France, Japan, Canada	Versailles Summit: short-lived monetary accord
May 1983	United States, West Germany, United Kingdom, Italy, France, Japan, Canada	Williamsburg Summit: East-West economic issues and no change in American economic policies
June 1984	United States, West Germany, United Kingdom, Italy, France, Japan, Canada	London Summit (tenth summit): complaints against American twin deficits; Declaration on Democratic Values
September–October 1984	West Germany and others	Independent action by central banks to drive dollar down; upward movement of dollar by late October
January 1985	Group of Five	Commitment to coordinate market intervention when needed
February 1985	United States	Federal Reserve Chairman Volcker's statement that intervention could play a role in financial system
March 1985	United States, Japan, West Germany,	Large coordinated market intervention to force dollar down
May 1985	United States, West Germany, United Kingdom, Italy, France, Japan, Canada	Bonn Summit
September 1985	Group of Five	Plaza Agreement to drive dollar down
October–November 1985	Group of Five	Official determination to coordinate action to drive dollar down
December 1985	United States	The signing into law of Gramm-Rudman-Hollings

TABLE 6.1
Continued

Date	Alliance nations	Action taken
January 1986	Group of Five	Announcement that further decline of dollar would not be unacceptable
March 1986	United States, West Germany, Japan, France	Coordination of downward movement of discount rates
April 1986	United States, Japan	Coordination of downward movement of discount rates
May 1986	United States, West Germany, United Kingdom, Italy, France, Japan, Canada	Tokyo Summit: Economic indicator surveillance plan
September 1986	Group of Five and Group of Seven	Agreement that "cooperative efforts should be intensified"
October 1986	United States, Japan	Baker-Miyazawa Accord
December 1986	United States, West Germany	Baker-Stoltenberg meeting
January 1987	United States, Japan	Baker-Miyazawa meeting; joint statement
February 1987	Group of Five and Group of Seven	Louvre Accord, meeting boycotted by Italy
June 1987	United States, West Germany, United Kingdom, Italy, France, Japan, Canada	Venice Summit: reaffirmation of Louvre Accord and the Washington agreements
September 1987	Group of Seven	Agreement that "currencies are within ranges broadly consistent with . . . fundamentals"
October 1987		Stock market crash
December 1987	Group of Seven	Emphasis on common interest in exchange market and macroeconomic stability

Sources: Based on BIS (various years); Dobson (1991); Funabashi (1989); Putnam and Bayne (1984); Solomon (1982).

The Movement toward Cooperation in the 1970s

The first effort to restore order to the international financial system after the Nixon shocks of 1971 took place at the Smithsonian Institution in Washington, D.C., in December 1971. The Smithsonian Agreement in the short term sought to restore order and confidence to the international financial system and in the longer term to promote the adjustment of American payments imbalances with surplus countries (BIS, 1972–73:20). The agreement reestablished a degree of order to international finance by removing the American import surcharge imposed the previous August, devaluing the American dollar by 7.9 percent to allow more accurate exchange rates among the major currencies and revaluing a number of other currencies as well (BIS, 1971–72:29). Unfortunately, the agreement fell short of what American officials perceived as necessary to restore a substainable balance in the American external accounts (Solomon, 1982:215), even though President Nixon referred to it as "the most significant monetary agreement in the history of the world" (Williamson, 1977:8).

Ultimately, even though the allies recognized, and were willing to act on, the need for the American devaluation (and the subsequent strengthening of the American competitive position), the reconstituted fixed-rate system of the Smithsonian Agreement was in fact completely abandoned for freely floating rates in March 1973. A primary reason for this was that American domestic policies did not support the new rates. Even concerted official efforts by the allies during the summer of 1972 to maintain exchange rates (Solomon, 1982:391) could not forestall the real devaluation of the American dollar—at least partly due to expansionary Federal Reserve policies—on international markets during 1972 (BIS, 1972–73:25), thus demonstrating the futility of maintaining the fixed-rate mechanism under existing international conditions. From this time onward, a sentiment existed that Japan and West Germany would be required to make large contributions to the adjustment process in the new financial system (ibid., 28; Bergsten, 1975:386).

Throughout this early period, the Committee of Twenty of the IMF continued to focus on monetary reform but with little success.[6] As a result, the market became the reformed "system"—or really, nonsystem—as it relieved the pressure of unrealistic exchange rates, even though it produced a great deal of volatility within the system (BIS, 1973–74:27). This de-facto reformation, however, did not preclude efforts to manage the volatility of the system by the major currency countries. In particular, at the monthly meeting of central bank governors in July 1973, it was announced that arrangements were in place to allow for coordinated official intervention to restore an orderly financial market. In that spirit, the U.S. Federal Reserve and the West German Bundesbank intervened in financial markets in the same month to strengthen the dollar. It was generally felt that the dollar had depreciated below market equilibrium levels. Similar operations were carried out by the same authorities later in 1973 and early in 1974 (ibid., 29, 32).

But even though action was taken to stem the short-term variation and continued fall of the dollar between 1973 and 1975, the dollar remained weak through the mid-1970s, at least partially due to the increasing value of oil imports following the first oil shock (BIS, 1974–75:28). Coordinated action was taken in February 1975 to push the dollar's value upward: American, West German, and Swiss officials agreed in London to intervene on behalf of the dollar to maintain market order (Solomon, 1982:393). There was seemingly no Japanese role in the adjustment process, but considering the stability of the yen on international financial markets during this period, this is not surprising (BIS, 1974–75:27).

In the background, the Committee of Twenty continued to work on international monetary reform. By June 1974, this committee produced an outline of reform that set forth a more structured international monetary system than would emerge in later years (Solomon, 1982:263–66). The outline, though, fell far short of the committee's initial objective of "writing a new monetary constitution" (Williamson, 1977:73). Beyond the actual tenets of the committee's proposal, the report provided only a code of good behavior for participants in the floating exchange rate system. More precisely, the committee asserted that short-term disruptions of exchange rates within financial markets were to be smoothed by the players and that resistance should be offered to longer-term trends away from equilibrium (BIS, 1974–75:30). So although the committee attempted to reimpose structure onto monetary affairs, its efforts are more appropriately interpreted as the beginnings of guidelines for international monetary management. Certainly, the cooperative interventions in early 1975 and the outcomes of the Rambouillet Summit later in 1975 followed in the spirit, if not the letter, of the committee's wishes.[7]

The Rambouillet Summit of November 1975 was a turning point for Western cooperation in a number of ways. Held at the initiative of French President Valéry Giscard d'Estaing and West German Chancellor Helmut Schmidt, this summit was the beginning of the increasingly regularized process of Western summitry and, more specifically, of efforts to coordinate policy. The participants at Rambouillet issued an endorsement of floating rates and called upon the IMF to survey the rates. The governments also committed their central banks to intervene in currency markets to maintain order, called for macroeconomic policies to counter the recessionary trends of the mid-1970s, and called for completion of the Tokyo Round of GATT negotiations (Madison, 1983:1173).

But even though the principal legacy of the summit were its monetary achievements, their implementation fell short of the intentions of the summit. Although a complex system for consultation among the six participants was created—"daily between central banks, weekly between senior finance ministry officials, and quarterly between finance ministers"—the success of policy coordination also depended upon a sense in the markets that the authorities were committed to exchange rate stability (Putnam and Bayne, 1984:31, 33). So while Rambouillet can be considered a procedural and institutional success, it did not provide specific guidelines for the six nations beyond the public pronouncements on coordination (Cohen, 1977:120–21).[8] The achievements of Rambouillet were, therefore, the first tentative steps by the large Western nations to move toward cooperation under floating rates. The next two summits—in Puerto Rico in 1976 and in London in 1977—did little to solidify the operational side of cooperation but did demonstrate the allies' long-term commitment to high-level consultation and cooperation.

The operational shortfall of Rambouillet was clear over the next two years, as exchange markets remained volatile. During 1976, major disturbances occurred in the markets, and the strong and weak currencies became further polarized in value. Interestingly enough, the dollar remained relatively stable during that year, even though the American balance of payments further deteriorated (BIS, 1976–77:121). Conversely, 1977 was a less volatile year overall for exchange rates but, coincidentally, witnessed a substantial fall of the dollar from about June to early 1978 (ibid.; BIS, 1977–78:111). More important from the view of Western cooperation, the fluctuations experienced during this period seem to provide the impetus for more active coordinated operational action.

By early 1978 a greater commitment to coordinated intervention was in evidence. In February 1978, Japan, West Germany, Switzerland, and the United States engaged in substantial coordinated operations to strengthen the dollar. This was followed in April and May by similar actions on the part of the Japanese, Germans, and Americans, which successfully pushed the value of the dollar upward (BIS, 1977–78:112–13; Solomon, 1982:395). These actions and the underlying tenets of coordinated action were further supported by the developments of the July 1978 Bonn Summit.

Proclaimed by French President Giscard d'Estaing as ushering in a "new era of mutual trust among the seven" (Putnam and Bayne, 1984:95), the Bonn Summit not only produced a stronger commitment to exchange rate surveillance and coordinated intervention but, more generally, placed coordination of macroeconomic policies onto the menus of the seven (Funabashi, 1989:37). Just before the summit, Japanese Prime Minister Fukuda honored his pledge to stimulate the Japanese economy. He also announced that Japan would hold its export volume constant that year, implement an "emergency" import program, and double its foreign assistance. France announced that it would undertake a budgetary expansion. A German stimulus program was also enunciated and later approved by the German cabinet in special session. Similar commitments to Western economic recovery were given by Italy, Canada, and the United Kingdom, though their policies were in place prior to the summit (Putnam and Bayne, 1984:91–93; Solomon, 1982:313–14). Add to these actions President Carter's anti-inflationary package and we get a picture of a reasonably harmonious Western summit, making progress toward macroeconomic coordination and financial stability.

Counter to many earlier cases, the commitment to coordination and stability endured after the summit, and the leaders generally delivered on the promises made at Bonn (Ilgen, 1985:129). Even though many in the private sector doubted the reality of coordination or its potential for endurance, these doubts were eliminated by the action taken by monetary authorities in the fall of 1978. In October and November, American and Swiss authorities took action to stabilize both the dollar and the exchange markets. Those actions were followed by activity in November by the Americans and the Swiss in conjunction with the Germans and the Japanese: swap lines were increased among the four countries, with the Japanese, Germans, and Swiss making substantial purchases of dollars. Moreover, the United States announced a large-scale intervention to strengthen the dollar, issued $10 billion of U.S. government securities valued in foreign currencies, and raised the discount rate by 1 percent. These actions were so successful that by March 1979, the same countries had to intervene to maintain exchange rates against the dollar (BIS, 1978–79:134–37; 1979–80:134).

These actions demonstrated that American officials had changed their philosophy toward market intervention and policy coordination and were willing to cooperate with other authorities, notably the Japanese, German, and Swiss, to control the exaggerated swings in exchange values. The stability witnessed in foreign exchange markets from 1978 until the second oil shock in 1980 was a direct result of these coordinated interventions.[9] Not only did these policies help stabilize the markets, they also instilled confidence in the private sector regarding the willingness and ability of authorities to manage exchange markets (BIS, 1978–79:149; 1979–80:133–34, 143–44).

In terms of burden sharing, in the 1978–80 period, some of the burden of adjustment shifted away from the United States, although the United States still played a central role. The fact that exchange market stability was not achieved until American authorities actively coordinated intervention is evidence of the continued need for American participation in international finance. Nonetheless, even in the absence of an American role, the allies were inclined to stabilize markets on their own. This period also witnessed increasing independent action by the Europeans. It was not until the Bonn Summit, however, that consensus over a policy course was obtained among the larger allies. Unfortunately, an American inclination toward cooperation in international financial management would prove short lived as the Reagan administration came into office in 1981 and retreated to a more extreme version of the pre-1978 American free-market stance. So while cooperation and burden sharing emerged in 1978 among the allies, the allies would not truly appreciate the meaning of macroeconomic burdens until the dollar began to soar and the American twin deficits ballooned in the early 1980s, causing widespread changes in the Western macroeconomic situation.

The Engine of Recovery or Dangerous Disequilibrium?

Ronald Reagan came into office espousing market-oriented economic policies. On the domestic scene, this meant the privatization of many functions long under the government umbrella. On the international scene, this meant faith in the ability of exchange markets to decide the value of the dollar with no government intervention at all. Operationally, these concepts were implemented through a monetarist tight money policy—begun by the Federal Reserve in the late 1970s—aimed at lowering inflation, cutting taxes, cutting spending in some government sectors (the major exception being defense), with nonintervention in international financial markets, or what Thomas Ilgen (1985:133) called "benign neglect."

In essence, the consensus over the benefits of market intervention and macroeconomic policy coordination that emerged during the late 1970s fell apart largely because of the policy changes instituted by the Reagan administration. In the administration's clearest statement of policy toward international finance, U.S. Treasury Secretary Donald Regan announced in April 1981 that the United States would not regularly intervene in foreign exchange markets (Solomon, 1982:398; BIS, 1981–82:154). The value of the dollar soared in foreign exchange markets because of high American interest rates, political uncertainty in Europe (especially in France and Germany) and the Middle East, and the impression that the American economy was a safe haven for capital at least in the short term (Marris, 1987:24, 30–32). In the first year of the Reagan administration (January 1981 to April 1982), the dollar increased 26 percent in value, as foreign capital gravitated to the American market. Moreover, the dollar's value was not the only concern in financial circles, since without the tool of official intervention to smooth out the wrinkles, the dollar was much more volatile over shorter time periods (BIS, 1981–82:141). Such volatility produces the long-term problems and uncertainty outlined at the beginning of this chapter.

But what was not known was that the dollar had only begun to increase in value and would not peak until February 1985. Throughout the early 1980s, the policies adopted by the allies—particularly the United States—were not primarily aimed at producing economic stability for the alliance as a whole. In its report published in June 1981 (the 1980–81 report), the Bank for International Settlements recommended that the United States and other countries should ease monetary policies, tighten fiscal policies, and reduce interest rates (Solomon, 1982:357). In the United States, just the opposite was in fact the case: a tight monetary policy was instituted to fight inflation, and the largest fiscal expansion in American history was under way. The BIS in the following year's report also recommended greater multilateral coordination of exchange rate policies so that the instability in the exchange market of the previous two years could be controlled (BIS, 1982–83:137). Given this economic situation and the perceived demands of the revitalized Cold War in the United States, it was inevitable that the United States and the allies would be at odds during the early 1980s. The U.S. perception of threat drew attention away from the economic issues and relationships that had become increasingly important to the allies during the 1970s era of détente.

The Western summits from 1981 to 1984 illustrate the coordination of alliance policies and the distribution of the monetary burdens among the allies. At each of the four summits, high American interest rates and the effects they were having on the European and Japanese economies was an important issue. In later years, the budget deficit took center stage both at the summits and throughout the year, because it was perceived as a central cause of the continuation of high interest rates and the American current account deficit. The American deficit and high interest rates were also blamed for delaying the recovery process in other industrialized countries (Ilgen, 1985:135).

The 1981 Ottawa Summit can best be characterized as nondecisional. Its inconclusiveness, however, actually minimized the differences between presidents Reagan and Mitterand. All parties came away from the summit stating that no changes were required in their own policies as a result of summit discussions (Putnam and Bayne, 1984:158; Madison, 1983:1173). The implications of this summit, however, are most clearly stated by Robert Putnam and Nicholas Bayne: "In a world without interdependencies, this sort of congenial 'live and let live' anarchy could ensure international comity. However, summitry had emerged precisely because the modern world is not so simple as that. Before they met next in Versailles, each leader would be reminded that achieving his own purposes required cooperation from the others, cooperation that would prove elusive" (1984:158). As this implies, the following year's Versailles Summit differed significantly from the Ottawa Summit in that the disagreements among the seven were more obvious, giving it the dubious notoriety of being the first "failed" summit.

This summit led to further polarization of the allies over East-West technology transfer issues and intervention in foreign exchange markets. The U.S. Treasury appeared convinced of the futility of intervention, while the French and others saw it as essential to collective monetary management. The monetary agreements hammered out at the summit fell apart within two weeks of the summit's end. At the heart of this failure was European resentment of American paternalism—Europeans might say arrogance—on technology transfer issues and American skepticism regarding the utility of monetary intervention and coordination (ibid., 163, 166–67, 170; Madison, 1983:1173).

The positive aura surrounding the 1983 Williamsburg Summit resulted from the progress of world economic recovery and also from the lower expectations of participants and observers after the 1982 Versailles outcome. Although little had changed in the American macroeconomic package and the allies continued to press the deficit and interest rates issues, pledges of economic policy coordination were once again a mainstay. The Williamsburg "success" was arrived at by avoidance of disagreements, not by actual policy change (Madison, 1983:1171; Putnam and Bayne, 1984:192–95). If nothing else, some of the accusations and recriminations that characterized Versaille and its aftermath had disappeared.

The 1984 London Summit witnessed the continued centrality of the twin-deficits problem, particularly as it pertained to allied accusations of American overstimulation of the world economy. Nonetheless, this summit also produced the Declaration on Democratic Values, affirming the seven nations' beliefs in freedom, equality, and progress

(Weisman, 1984). The declaration was significant from a rhetorical standpoint, as it was issued only eight months after the breakdown of the U.S.-Soviet arms control proceedings in November 1983. That walkout was the low point in East-West relations in the 1980s. And the declaration was evidence of the core Western values underlying even the most serious political and economic disputes. So although little of economic substance was decided upon in London, one began to see the reemergence of Western cooperation. This trend would be further solidified as the opinions and policies of the Reagan administration changed over the following year regarding the value of intervention.

From a burden-sharing perspective, a number of ideas pertaining to the monetary developments in the early 1980s should be kept in mind. First, one must not view the large American military budgets in the 1980s as simply another example of the disproportionate burdens borne by the United States in the military realm. The simple arithmetic of military spending masks the macroeconomic implications of that spending. The American defense budget expansion of the early 1980s was partly responsible for the high interest rates in the Western economies. While the Reagan administration was preaching—though not practicing—fiscal austerity on the domestic side—and was able to politically exploit the "tax and spend" image of the Democratic party—many in the United States lost sight of the fiscal expansion in the military realm.

American fiscal expansion and the attendant macroeconomic trends of capital flight from abroad to the United States and exchange market volatility are not the only parts of the burden-sharing equation. The American budget deficit also forced the allies to bear some of the costs of alliance military defense, although greater costs will likely be be borne by the American taxpayers of the future. This situation is similar to David Calleo's (1982) argument regarding alliance relationships, the American balance of payments deficit, and the exporting of American inflation under the Bretton Woods system in the 1960s. Certainly, the fact that allies continually pointed to the budget deficit as the source of many of their own macroeconomic problems suggests that they were bearing some significant costs—albeit unwillingly—and that the Reagan administration was, early in the 1980s, unwilling to ease those burdens. International cooperation was not possible with the American policy mix.

A second set of costs borne by the allies is also evident in the political relationships that developed in the late 1970s and the changes ushered in in 1981. By 1978 a basic consensus had emerged among the G-7 countries on the need for macroeconomic policy coordination and active intervention policies in exchange markets. This consensus emerged largely due to changes in Carter's policies. Policy change is natural when governments change, but the extent of change brought in by the Reagan administration in the realm of international economics is striking, especially given the tentative consensus that had emerged within the alliance after 1978. These problems were exacerbated by the unilateral foreign policy tendencies of the Reagan administration. From a lack of consultation on the Grenadan invasion to Secretary Regan's return to market policies and his abrasive diplomacy, the Reagan administration made negative contributions to the alliance effort during this period.

Curiously enough, during a period of renewed East-West hostilities and a time when traditional alliance theory would posit that an alliance should exhibit greater coherence, the alliance actually was more in disarray than at any other time in recent history. The disarray was caused not only by Reagan policies, however; it had its roots in the divergence of allied nation security perceptions. But while these divergent security interests could have been used to spur greater specialization and security trade within the alliance, they were taken by some American officials as evidence of a lack of commitment to the alliance on the part of some allies. This was one reason for the disagreement of the Versailles Summit over technology transfer. Therefore, Reagan's early and narrow-minded pursuit of security in the military realm detracted from alliance security. In other words, early Reagan macroeconomic policies, the policy changes away from coordination and consultation, and the unilateral decisionmaking tendencies produced negative American contributions politically and economically, given the costs of these policies perceived by the allies.

The Rebirth of Cooperation under Interdependence

Yoichi Funabashi identified the politics of American policy change thus:

> Although members of Congress wanted the depreciation of the dollar, there was a considerable psychological block against currency depreciation, especially after the years of the Reagan administration's preaching that a strong dollar represented a strong America.
>
> To President Ronald Reagan, the Plaza Agreement demonstrated continuity in policy, not change. Certainly "the President supported the Plaza strategy" and "was very pleased with the reaction around the world, and the aftermath of the Plaza," a Reagan administration official later remarked. But a new strategy had to be depicted as an extension, not as a departure from or alternative to the formal policy. (1989:65)

Specifically, the American policy change manifested in the signing of the Plaza Agreement by the Group of Five (G-5) and the following efforts at policy coordination resulted from a confluence of American domestic political developments. Most significant of these developments was James Baker's move from White House chief of staff to treasury secretary at the start of 1985. Donald Regan was the other participant in the swap. Baker—in contrast to Regan and his experience in the Wall Street financial scene—came to the treasury job with few preconceived notions about international finance. But as domestic political forces began to put pressure on Congress and the White House to do something about the ballooning trade deficit, Baker's strategy became one of forestalling the protectionist sentiments of Congress and the American people by moving toward a policy of dollar depreciation and, ultimately, cooperative intervention and policy coordination among the G-5 and G-7 countries (ibid., 75–76). The United States finally faced the fact that the high dollar was damaging American industrial competitiveness.

Baker's job, then, became one of selling this policy change to the president, to Federal Reserve Chairman Paul Volcker, and to Secretary of State George Schultz (a free-market economist by trade). The selling job was particularly tricky given the strong dollar/strong America image noted in the quotation above and also because of the president's personal commitment to that image (ibid., 76). But once the major domestic players were sold on the need for a new dollar strategy and for greater cooperation with the allies in managing their interdependencies, the process got under way. The allies announced in January 1985 that coordinated intervention would be undertaken when needed. Nonetheless, even though a more constructive G-5 and G-7 process was emerging, the American deficit would still loom as a problem for alliance cooperation in the years ahead.

What emerged as American policy in early 1985—coordinated intervention—had already taken hold in allied governments. In September and October 1984 the Bundesbank and other central banks undertook seemingly independent actions to drive the dollar down. Success was elusive, as the dollar moved up again by late October. It was not until the Americans came on board that the strategy of driving the dollar began to show signs of working over the longer term. On 17 January 1985, at a G-5 meeting of finance ministers and central bank governors, it was announced that coordinated intervention would be used when needed (ibid., 249). This was followed in February with statements by Federal Reserve Chairman Volcker that forceful intervention could play a role in international finance. These statements led in turn to coordinated official interventions in February and March, with American participation much greater than it had been previously. Although foreign exchange markets remained unsettled through much of the spring of 1985, the policy change had its effects, as the dollar peaked in value against both the yen and the deutsche mark at the end of February (BIS, 1984–85:143; Funabashi, 1989:249).

In August 1985, however, the dollar rebounded sharply on financial markets, once again raising protectionist sentiments in Congress. These international and domestic pressures were a spur to the G-5 Plaza Agreement of September 1985. As a result of the instability of financial markets throughout 1985 and also the summer rebound of the dollar, G-5 finance ministers and central bank governors once again agreed to coordinate market intervention, now also aimed at accelerating the decline of the dollar (Dobson, 1991:41). The strategy also aimed to achieve these goals through the orderly appreciation of other currencies. This event saw the issuance of the first statement in which the G-5 countries, and in particular the United States, identified the American twin deficits of budget and trade as a world problem. Public announcements and private agreements were followed up in October and November with shows of official determination for coordinated action relating to the dollar (BIS, 1985–86:144). Nonetheless, the Plaza communiqué avoided the word *intervention* and did not focus on dollar depreciation. It focused on the appreciation of other currencies, thus deflecting blame from the United States.

Another show of commitment to cooperative economic management came from the United States in December with the passage of the Gramm-Rudman-Hollings deficit reduction program (Funabashi, 1989:249). Although it would not eliminate the problem, the law was evidence that the American government was finally moving toward fiscal restraint, limited though it was. At the multilateral level, in January 1986 the G-5 continued its assault on the dollar's value by announcing that further depreciation of the dollar would not be unacceptable. The "talking the dollar down" strategy was followed first in March by coordinated downward moves of discount rates in the United States, West Germany, Japan, and France and, subsequently, additional downward discount rate moves in the United States and Japan in April. In the spirit of continual and close consultation, these events were supported by meetings throughout the period among finance ministers, finance deputies, and also central bank officials (BIS, 1985–86:146–47; Funabashi, 1989:250). In other words, once a consensus was reached among the allies on the value of coordination in late

1984 and early 1985, policy coordination was actively, if not always successfully, pursued.

Policy coordination was expanded still further at the Western summit in Tokyo when a multilateral economic surveillance plan was adopted by the G-7 as a way of monitoring macroeconomic developments among the Western nations. Included in the plan were such indicators as GNP growth, interest rates, budget deficit as a percentage of GNP, growth of the money supply, exchange rates, inflation and unemployment rates, current account and trade balances, and foreign exchange reserves (Dobson, 1991:49). This method for cooperative economic management was intended to identify macroeconomic developments that would have potentially detrimental effects on the health of Western nations though it would not become a terribly useful tool because of a lack of consensus on the weighting of the indicators.

Operationally, the surveillance plan was used to apply peer pressure on particular governments. Wendy Dobson (1991) identified two major instances where peer pressure was used to promote domestic policy change. First, in 1986 and early 1987 the United States pressured the Japanese into stimulating domestic demand to help the United States rectify its deficit problems. Similar pressure was applied to Germany in 1987 and 1988 (74). The logic was for countries with surpluses to stimulate domestic demand to provide a larger market for American goods (both by increased consumer demand and by putting inflationary pressure on their own currencies, making their own goods more expensive internationally). In terms of burden sharing, this pressure ran counter to the inclination of the Germans and the Japanese, which was to emphasize austere fiscal policies and control inflation (Rowen, 1987). For the Germans, economic stimulation usually came from the supply side, so demand stimulation was a unique policy course for them (Dobson, 1991:74).

Throughout 1986 and early 1987, high-level contacts, particularly among U.S., Japanese, and German officials, was intensive. Three weeks after the Tokyo Summit, the G-5 deputies had a follow-up meeting on the indicator surveillance plan. In September 1986, after some initial European misgivings about the continued fall of the dollar, the G-7 met in Washington and stated that coordinated efforts should be intensified. In October came the Baker-Miyazawa Accord, which "traded assurances by Japan to cut the discount rate and initiate tax reform for those by the United States to stop depreciating the dollar" (Funabashi, 1989:53). In December, Baker met with German Finance Minister Gerhard Stoltenberg and discussed German demand stimulation along with domestic constraints on policy decisions in both countries. More than anything else, this meeting laid the groundwork for the Louvre Accord of February 1987 and also helped solidify G-3 cooperation that had been emerging over the past two years (172–73).

The constraints on the German ability to stimulate its economy were evident when the German discount rate was raised in January 1987. This in addition to the contractionary fiscal policies of Germany and Japan led to a further drop of the dollar on international markets (BIS, 1986–87:155). Because of the dollar's drop, Japanese and American officials jointly intervened to support the dollar on 28 January, producing a symbolic as well as a real initiative aimed at demonstrating multilateral commitment. This was the first time the United States had intervened to defend a floor for the dollar. It also led to speculation that another G-5 meeting was in the making, speculation that proved valid when the meeting took place on 21–22 February (BIS, 1986–87:156–57; Funabashi, 1989:252).

Aside from the Italian upset over its and Canada's exclusion from the first day of meetings, the Louvre meeting was a success in institutionalizing coordination of exchange rate management and macroeconomic policies, even if not in propping up the dollar's value. The intervention policies undertaken since the Plaza Agreement had demonstrated that the G-5 nations could cooperate in this area, but the longer-term outcome of the Plaza meeting was that it also demonstrated the need to go beyond simply coordinating market interventions. As the Bank for International Settlements stated a year after the Louvre Accord, the accord makes clear that internationally coordinated exchange intervention can be especially successful in maintaining exchange market stability if combined with appropriate domestic macroeconomic policy changes (BIS, 1987–88:175), such as American fiscal deficit reduction.

From a burden-sharing standpoint, the Louvre Accord shows that the allies were cajoled into helping the United States deal with macroeconomic problems that were largely of American doing. The G-5 decided to maintain exchange rates "around current levels," even though the Japanese wanted those "current levels" to mean some appreciation of the dollar against the yen (Funabashi, 1989:186). Although an explicit establishment of exchange rate target zones was problematic because of the threat of private sector speculation, the arrangements and rates would still be benchmarks for future interventions. Moreover, Japan and West Germany were pressed to make domestic stimulation efforts. Given German domestic politics, stimulation through tax reform would prove difficult, although speeding up the planned 1988 tax cuts was proposed. The fall 1987 stock market crash would ultimately provide more political fuel for German decisionmakers in this area (Dobson, 1991:83–84; Funabashi, 1989:196).

For the Japanese, domestic economic stimulation was more forthcoming, though it was not the policy of choice from a domestic political vantage point. Part of the reason that the Japanese were more inclined to undertake such policies was their relatively larger trade stake in the health of the American economy. This was especially relevant given that the American economy had been the engine for recovery in the early to mid-1980s. The Japanese government adopted a supplemental budget in April 1987 aimed at stimulating economic activity and import purchases (BIS, 1987–88:167). Additional fiscal expansion efforts would come later that year.

Both Japan and Germany were then pushed to adopt policies somewhat outside their preferred policy mixes, at least partially because American policymakers were unable (or unwilling) to shrink the fiscal deficit. As would continue to be the case over the months and years ahead, the American budget deficit was an animal out of the control of the G-5, even though it had significant effects on the relationships among the Western countries. As Yoichi Funabashi concluded, "the Louvre Accord was the product of ad hoc political imperatives and, above all, the political needs of the United States" (1989:202).

The budget deficit theme and the needs for stimulation outside the United States would be heard over and over again. At the Venice Summit in June 1987, the G-7 reaffirmed the essentials of the Louvre Accord and defended the current exchange rates, stating that further shifts could be counterproductive to growth. The continued validity of the Louvre Accord was supported again at a meeting of finance ministers and central bank governors in September 1987, when they stated that "currencies are within ranges broadly consistent with . . . fundamentals" (BIS, 1987–88:167, 169; Dobson, 1991:65).

In some ways, the greatest threat to public and private faith in the continuation of policy coordination came in October 1987 with the worldwide stock market crash. Nonetheless, the Bank for International Settlements asserted that the basic concepts of the Louvre Accord did not contribute to this event but, rather, that it was caused by the individual national policies that could have given the Louvre Accord more operational weight. In particular, the bank pointed to the need for greater American fiscal restraint and stronger stimulation efforts by Japan and West Germany (BIS, 1987–88:177).

And although the empirical time frame for this study ends more or less with 1987, the policy coordination process evident since 1985 and more broadly since 1987 continued. It is increasingly clear that the "Plaza process" has become an integral part of Western cooperation.

Moreover, no mention was made of exchange rates in the statements from the 1989 Paris Summit or the 1990 Houston Summit (Dobson, 1991:66). A number of explanations for this development are plausible. First, and probably most significantly, the coordination process had become so much a part of the roles of the finance ministers, their deputies, and central bank officials that the high-level attention given these issues at earlier Western summits was no longer essential. In other words, coordination became normal and did not require heads of government to sanction policy in the same way they are required to sanction policy changes.

Second, particularly at the Houston Summit, the problems and controversies relating to the fall of the Soviet bloc occupied much of the leaders' time. As a result, the summits are used to discuss and debate the hotter issues, not policy implementation. Continued Western preoccupation with the issue of Soviet aid at the 1991 London Summit is a case in point. Third, 1988 and 1989 were relatively stable years in the foreign exchange markets, and the success of policy coordination placed the issue of exchange markets on the back burner, politically. Policy cooperation in Western security affairs, though not perfect, has produced greater confidence in the abilities of the allies to control their collective economic destinies.[10] Last, the EMS has provided added stability for Europeans, especially in the event of a skewed dollar value.

The Long and Winding Road

Burden sharing among the Western allies in the international monetary realm is not as tangibly measured as military expenditures, foreign aid, and research and development, but a general picture can be obtained of the types of contributions and costs borne by particular allies in their efforts to serve common security goals. The desire for monetary stability in the immediate aftermath of the fall of Bretton Woods led to cooperative efforts for maintaining stability and to the creation and institutionalization of the Western summit process. American policy changes in the early 1980s produced a situation that at times was quite costly to allied economic health, and only when the American deficits problems became acute because of domestic political pressure on the Reagan administration did the United States cooperate with the allies to bring the dollar down and coordinate policies. Since that point, policy coordination and burden sharing in monetary affairs has been a qualified success. Clearly, the policies adopted by American allies during the latter half of the 1980s to help the United States rectify its deficit problems by adopting policies counter to their preferred political choices should be viewed as contributions to alliance security.

It was clear since the Plaza Agreement that depreciation of the dollar alone could not stabilize the world economy. The subsequent allied cooperative efforts had a noticeable impact: The American current account deficit declined, the American budget deficit decreased from 5 percent of GNP in 1987 to 3 percent of GNP in 1989, the dollar depreciated after 1985 and stabilized by the end of 1987, and American demand slowed, while Japanese and German demand picked up (Dobson, 1991:131). All in all, these efforts achieved many of the national and collective goals of the major Western nations. In contrast to traditional realist conceptions of security policy, Western cooperation in the areas discussed demonstrates that national interests need not always dictate international cooperation. Rather, cooperation and collective action can become part of a long-term strategy of mutually beneficial collective arrangements, and at times the short-term, narrow national interests will be subordinated.

Dollar instability and American unilateralism (or at least its ignoring of the alliancewide implications of policy change) at times imposed significant costs on the allies. In this sense, the United States made negative contributions to alliance security. As for the United Kingdom, France, Italy, and Canada, their roles were important in the late 1980s but were not as central to adjustment efforts as those of the two main surplus countries, Japan and Germany. France, for instance, vowed at the Plaza, the Louvre, and again in December 1987 to curb its public expenditure and reduce taxes. Similar pledges were made by Canada and the United Kingdom. Italy pledged in the December 1987 G-7 communiqué that it would correct its public imbalances and stabilize its debt-GDP ratio (Dobson, 1991:82–85). In each case, these countries undertook policies in coordination with the big three G-7 members.

For earlier years, the contributions were less tangible but, nonetheless, important to the overall political framework of alliance cooperation, as each of these countries helped get the summit process off the ground. They absorbed their share of the costs of the fall of Bretton Woods and of American unilateral policy, as well. French President Giscard d'Estaing is the "undisputed initiator" of the summit process (Putnam and Bayne, 1984:21); the French role was central to the atmosphere of cooperation that emerged between the United States and the Europeans in the mid to late 1970s. In fact, the monetary accord of the Rambouillet Summit, though short-lived, was crafted cooperatively by the French and Americans at the start of the summit (Putnam and Bayne, 1984:31; Williamson, 1977:73).

The European monetary system (EMS) also played an important role in these affairs. The main international concern of Bundesbank officials was to safeguard the currency relationships of the EMS (Funabashi, 1989:58). In contrast to the Japanese, who were almost solely concerned with yen-dollar ratios, the Germans had two priorities in monetary negotiations. The monetary burdens of France and Italy were similar though not as extensive outside the EMS as the German burdens were. Ultimately, the EMS gave the Europeans added protection against counterproductive dollar trends.

In the end, the monetary portion of alliance security cooperation has not been significantly skewed toward the United States, at least since the fall of Bretton Woods. Instead, the United States, while still the central variable in the equation of policy coordination and alliance macroeconomic health, must nonetheless rely on its allies to maintain system stability and even to fix economic problems of its own making. Moreover, in terms of policy flexibility, the United States is the only alliance nation that can refrain from cooperation with its allies at least in the short term.[11] This implies that the United States is able to impose short-term costs on its allies to a much larger degree than they can reciprocate without jeopardizing their own economic health and security. In the big picture of monetary burden sharing, then, the United States has little to complain about regarding the contributions made by its allies.

7

The Future of the Western Alliance System

THE THREAT that held the Western alliance together since 1949 disappeared in 1989, when the alliance's former adversaries gave up their totalitarian ways and focused their energy on their own internal problems. Many analysts now question whether the alliance can survive in this less confrontational international environment (Kirkpatrick, 1990; Safire, 1988; Mearsheimer, 1990a, 1990b; Kondracke, 1990; Sloan, 1990; Pick, 1990; Riding, 1990; Steel, 1990; Cheung et al., 1990; Vatikiotis, 1990).[1]

It is certainly true that the movement of the Soviet Union from ally to adversary in the immediate postwar era was the primary reason for the formation of NATO in 1949 and the subsequent flurry of alliance formation during the Eisenhower-Dulles years.[2] From the misunderstandings of Yalta to Kennan's article X to NSC-68 and the rearmament of the United States and the allies, alliance decisionmakers were clearly concerned with a growing Soviet military threat, first on the European continent and later throughout the world. The communist takeover in China and the advent of a Soviet nuclear weapons capability further solidified the Western perception of a Soviet and communist threat to Western interests and ideals. Throughout the following forty years, the Soviet threat served a central, though somewhat cyclical, purpose for unity among the Western allies.

But to say that the alliance lost the glue that held it together, to borrow John Mearsheimer's (1990b) analogy, ignores the many facets of the alliance that go beyond the narrow mission of deterring Soviet military aggression. It also ignores the fact that, as one study asserted (Flanagan and Dunn, 1990:215), "crises have been a permanent feature of alliance history." An examination of the titles of books and articles dealing with the alliance shows that academics and policymak-

113

ers have at various times perceived that the alliance was in the midst of a crisis.[3] Beginning with the French withdrawal from NATO in 1966, significant cleavages have been evident within the alliance, but none of these has led to alliance disintegration. The rise of Willy Brandt's *ostpolitik* and the subsequent fall of détente in the United States demonstrates the distinctly different approaches toward the Soviet Union espoused by alliance members.

The Europeans continually pushed for American policies more in line with the comprehensive proposals of the 1967 *Harmel Report* (U.S. House of Representatives, 1987:x, xiv). The deployment of a new generation of nuclear missiles in Europe in the early 1980s illustrates the popular apprehension over the alliance's nuclear weapons policies and the potential for serious gaps between elite support and mass support for a nuclear alliance (Domke, Eichenberg, and Kelleher, 1987:395–97; Prins, 1989:195–96; U.S. House of Representatives, 1987:xii–xiv). The alliance survived each of these situations.

Moreover, those writing premature obituaries for the Western alliance because of Eastern bloc changes should realize that the primary reason for an alliance's creation is not necessarily the primary reason for its continuation. International relations are not static. Numerous changes have occurred in the alliance and the international system since 1949 that provide opportunities—as well as challenges—to the Western alliance system.

The centrality of the Soviet threat to the continued viability of the alliance is further suspect when one places alliance interests into the broader security context discussed throughout this book. The elimination of an overriding military threat takes away only one of the alliance's roles and consequently forces other and new concerns to the fore. One must consider whether the Soviet military threat has been replaced by other global and regional military threats. The heightened military threats in the Middle East and other Third World areas might be seen, cynically, as a boon for the U.S. Department of Defense, as it searched for new missions in the post–Cold War era. More seriously, one must also ask which alliance structures aside from the NATO military command (e.g., the G-7) remain effective forums for dealing with the nonmilitary challenges faced by the alliance.

In many respects, the primary threats to alliance solidarity and viability come not from losing the Soviet threat but from other problems, including the tendency for American decisionmakers to make policy decisions unilaterally on issues of multilateral importance, the potential for increased trade friction among the North Americans, Japan, and the European community, and the need for the rising

economic powers to assume international responsibilities commensurate with their status and power.[4] The successful resolution of each of
these problems is at least partially dependent upon resolving the other
two.

American unilateral decisionmaking tendencies become more dan-
gerous for the alliance as American capabilities for unilateral action
become more limited. But a great deal of optimism remains regarding
the future of the Western alliance and the tendency for collective
international management. The framework for Western cooperation
built over the years will play a significant role in smoothing out intra-
alliance differences. Simply put, the present crisis in the alliance is
not really new but is the manifestation of the sometimes bumpy and
winding road toward security cooperation in intra-alliance politics,
negotiations, and policy implementation. National policies may not
always be cooperative, but they are nonetheless based on a core of
common alliance interests that will remain reasonably stable in the
foreseeable future.

Theory and Practice in Western Alliance Affairs

Optimism for the future of Western alliance affairs comes not only
from evaluations of the ways the alliance has weathered past crises
and dealt with policy challenges but also from the theoretical and
conceptual ideas of multidimensional security cooperation presented
throughout this study. Blending the conceptual and theoretical points
of the early chapters with the empirical evidence of later ones demonstrates that the negative appraisals of narrowly focused models of
alliance security cooperation misguide expectations about the efficiency and equity of alliance security provision. They also downplay
the degree to which the alliance is capable of dealing with change and
of formulating cooperative solutions to collective problems.

The examination of alliance or national security as a single public
good neglects the diversity of factors that influence security in the
contemporary international system. For all nations, not only the members of the Western alliance system, security is defined across military,
economic, and political spheres. Nonmilitary security concerns became
particularly acute in the 1970s, forcing the Western alliance system
to formulate security strategies aimed not only at deterring military
aggression but at ensuring economic, political, and environmental
stability.[5] So although, as Susan Strange (1990:238–39) suggested, the
name of the international game changed from a territorial, strategic

one to an economically competitive one, the Western alliance has developed relationships capable of formulating and implementing coordinated economic policies.

Because of these changes, the analysis of collective security provision in the modern world must examine the record of provision of goods across the security policy spectrum. In the Western alliance system, this means determining the optimality of security provision by examining such categories as military expenditures, foreign aid donations, research and development expenditures, contributions to monetary stability, and many more. The more measures that can be identified as relevant to alliance security concerns, the more accurate the analysis.

Once we recognize that multiple public goods are being provided within the Western alliance, earlier theoretical constructs must be expanded to account for them and to provide a framework for the evaluation of the efficiency and equity of security provision. As presented here, this new framework for the analysis of international cooperation not only introduces considerations of multiple public goods to the model but brings the theoretical constructs used in the study of international cooperation closer to real-world approximations. In particular, this means explicitly stating that (1) allied nations consult with one another about their security policy decisions, (2) the multiple goods produced by the alliance are produced with varying degrees of efficiency by alliance members, and (3) the costs of production as perceived by allied decisionmakers not only are economic but are composed of political costs.

As shown in chapter 3, the introduction of any of these considerations to the public goods model provides, in addition to considerations of public goods impurity discussed by other analysts, an incentive for increased public goods provision. Placing these assumptions into a new framework for international cooperation provides a strong theoretical rationale for optimism when considering the prospects for successful achievement of international goals and objectives. From a substantive perspective, it also means that recent cooperative developments in Western affairs, such as the G-7 agreements and increasing Western attention to international debt problems, are not just isolated cases of cooperation but are, rather, the product of a broad-based alliance network, well suited for the pursuit of multiple security policy goals.

This new theory of international cooperation additionally posits that greater efficiency and equity in public goods production can be achieved through national specialization in the production of alliance goods along comparative advantage lines. An alliance nation that can produce military defense more efficiently than other alliance nations should devote its resources to the specialized production of military goods. Nations with comparative advantages in the production of economic goods, such as foreign aid or contributions to monetary stability, should specialize in the production of those goods. An alliance can increase its efficiency of production by trading these public goods within the alliance for other public goods or other private alliance goods (e.g., deficit financing during the 1980s for the United States).[6] Thus the critique in chapter 3 generates the hypothesis that alliance nations will specialize in the production of alliance goods for which they have a comparative advantage and trade these goods with other alliance nations. In other words, a division of security policy labor will occur among alliance members, further increasing alliance interreliance and interdependence.

In an alliance context where political stability is valued as highly as economic efficiency—or even more so—in the formulation of security policies, the concept of political comparative advantage must be incorporated into evaluations of the specialization possibilities possessed by alliance nations. In other words, to measure a particular nation's contribution to the alliance effort, one must be cognizant of the domestic political constraints on policymakers. Chapter 4 provides some indication of the political comparative advantages held by various alliance nations and suggests where and in what policy areas alliance burden sharing initiatives should be focused. For instance, the United States has an apparent political comparative advantage in military production, while Italy appears to have one in foreign aid. As a result of political comparative advantages, alliance nations must account for both political and economic factors when deciding upon security strategies, if the alliance is to maintain political solidarity and security from external threats, whether military, economic, or political.[7] As shown in the empirical portions of this study, Western nations have made distinct progress in the identification of political comparative advantages since the fall of the Bretton Woods system. The annual Western economic summits were established at least partly to help reconcile domestic economic pressures with international problems common to all (Putnam and Bayne, 1984:8). The summits have become a central forum for intra-alliance negotiations on domestic and international policy constraints.

Theoretical constructs are not all that point to Western alliance success. The empirical evidence in chapters 5 and 6 indicate that security burdens are more equitably distributed among the Western alliance countries than conventional wisdom asserts. In addition to the tendencies toward higher levels of alliance contributions resulting from the joint production of public and private goods, alliance nations do specialize in their alliance contributions in accord with their political and economic comparative advantages. Most alliance nations are free riders on one or more alliance security dimensions but bear heavier burdens on other dimensions. The United States, for instance, exhibits low contribution levels for foreign aid and benefits from the economic contributions of other G-7 nations such as Japan and Germany. These low contributions are balanced by high contributions to the military and R&D dimensions. The Japanese increased their foreign aid and made substantial contributions to monetary stability. Most other alliance nations exhibit specialization tendencies, as well.

Aside from apparent deviant cases, the evidence supports the hypotheses generated by our new public goods model of international cooperation. As a result, one can state that the alliance is a much more efficient organization than Olson and Zeckhauser's model suggests. Once multiple goods, differences in the relative economic and political costs of production, and consultation are introduced to the alliance model, it becomes clear that the alliance is not doing badly. Specialization of alliance contributions increases efficiency in the production of alliance goods and enhances alliance stability by promoting security interdependence among alliance members.

In terms of the future stability of the Western alliance, security policy specialization leads to increasing intra-alliance reliance for physical security, economic well-being, and political stability. This is not to say that existing specialization will not change—that once an ally specializes in military production, for example, it cannot reorient its policy priorities. It merely says that policy change within the alliance will be evolutionary rather than revolutionary. Policy stability is normal and expected. This is particularly true because minimum levels of security provision are required in all security realms, necessitating some degree of policy continuity, and because domestic rigidity in decisionmaking and security preferences tends to inhibit rapid change. But it should also be expected that the production constraints faced by all allies will shift over time to account for new domestic and international realities, thus producing pressures for policy change. Since 1971, the record of American cooperation in efforts to stabilize the international monetary system illustrates the slow response time of American foreign policy on this issue, even though the problems of market volatility had already been identified and acted upon by other allies.

Another example is useful for illustration. One of the worries of the American Left in the face of Persian Gulf problems was that the United States might become the world's mercenary force. The United States apparently assumed this role because of its military specialization, because of the vacuum left by Soviet international retrenchment, and because no other nation possessed the force projection capabilities necessary to play the role of world policeman. But this does not mean that the United States will and must maintain such a role indefinitely, although some in the American defense community would relish that development. In fact, the United States sought coalition involvement in the Persian Gulf military effort to deflect concern that the military operation was simply another example of American hegemony in the Middle East.

Cultivating greater non-American involvement in the future will be crucial to American policy success, as budgetary pressures continue to force cutbacks in American force projection capabilities. Proposals to strengthen the operational capabilities of the Western European Union would be a step in this direction. Moreover, since the start of the Gulf conflict there have been rumblings about changes in the German constitution to allow for out-of-area activities. A similar debate has been heard in Japan over its peacekeeping operations bill during 1991 and 1992. Almost monthly, some new military structure wrinkle is being proposed by someone within the alliance system. In fact, according to Elizabeth Sherwood's (1990) research, the basis for future alliance cooperation in out-of-area activities was being laid since 1949, though often behind the scenes or through the informal efforts of Western alliance diplomats. All this suggests that the United States may not remain relegated to military specialization, especially when one considers the demands for greater American fiscal responsibility and its impact on alliance (and American domestic) economic prosperity.

In addition, as the models of public goods provision presented in the appendixes demonstrate, changing relationships within the alliance also need not lead to decreased alliance efficiency. Both models point out that the dismal predictions of the hegemonic stability theorists regarding the future of Western cooperation are called into question when multiple goods and comparative advantage are introduced. As production frontiers move outward with the development of increased equality among alliance partners, these nations will be able to assume greater alliance burdens. This is especially true if national comparative advantages are identified and utilized within the alliance and if alliance goods are traded. The relative decline of American hegemony and the achievement by the allies of greater political and economic parity with the United States, therefore, are positive developments for Western alliance affairs.

This analysis does not imply that the alliance provides optimum security for its members but rather that it operates closer to optimum than a one-dimensional analysis of the alliance suggests. It does assert, however, that the alliance has made great strides toward optimality, especially since the downfall of the Bretton Woods system in the early 1970s. The theoretical constructs presented here yield insight into policy strategies that can improve alliance security while capitalizing on the diversity of interests among alliance nations. The models suggest that alliance policy should focus on uncovering the political and economic comparative advantages possessed by the various alliance countries and on promoting burden sharing in areas where particular nations have comparative advantages in production.

For instance, although Italy generally shows lower alliance contributions than some other alliance nations, the survey data in chapter 4 suggests that the Italian populace would support increases in Italian foreign aid.[8] Accordingly, if alliance members wish Italy to increase its alliance contributions, they should focus on promotion of Italy's foreign aid. Likewise, Japan may be able to make economic contributions to alliance security more easily than some other alliance nations. Thus Japan might make a political and economic contribution to the alliance by further opening its markets and promoting domestic purchase of foreign goods.

Across-the-board burden-sharing initiatives that attempt to force all nations to increase contributions on a particular alliance dimension are counterproductive for alliance efficiency. Proposals such as the 1984 Nunn Amendment, which would have mandated American troop withdrawals if the 3 percent spending increase goal was not met (*Congressional Record,* 1984), are politically divisive and unwise for overall alliance security concerns.[9] Burden-sharing initiatives, if they are to serve alliance security and promote greater Western cooperation, should be more discriminating in their goals. Without specialization, the alliance would operate farther from optimality than it does with specialization, because alliance nations would be forced to produce alliance goods in inefficient ways. Tailoring burden-sharing initiatives to fit comparative advantages provides the alliance with the opportunity to enhance international security rather than detract from it by pushing allies in undesirable policy directions.

The theory points to an increasingly interdependent alliance system that will focus on the ways individual nations can use their unique political and economic capabilities to serve both national and collective interests. Political comparative advantages ensure that national interest will be followed but also provides for the specialized production of alliance goods by individual countries. Until the commonalities of Western values and security concerns disappear, externalities will continue to be produced by national policy decisions. These externalities, whether purely public or not, yield benefits for all who hold the core Western values dear.

The most lasting legacy of American leadership in the early postwar period—and before that British leadership—and of the historical ties between the North American and European continents is the inculcation of common liberal economic and democratic values throughout the Western alliance system. Whether one should term this cultural hegemony or the *American vision* depends largely on one's perception of the motives of American decisionmakers in the postwar period. A number of studies challenged the forecasts of systemic instability produced by American decline on the grounds that the inculcation of Western values provided the basis for the development of political commonalities throughout the industrialized world. Joseph Nye (1990) referred to the long-term legacy of American power in the world as "soft power" and saw it as a positive influence on international stability in the years ahead. G. Ikenberry and Charles Kupchan (1990) challenged the conclusions of hegemonic stability theory by suggesting that, because other powers in the system are socialized into the dominant power's approach to international affairs, hegemonic decline does not necessarily lead to the immediate decay of international cooperation (315). Henry Nau (1990) made a similar argument about the effects of American ideals in the world as he made his case for freer and more liberal domestic and international economic systems. And Robert Wolfe (1990–91) stated the argument more strongly: "Atlanticism is an organizing principle that helps us see a pattern in a set of shared expectations among the participating countries" (138). In concluding his argument, he asserted that "the norms and principles of Atlanticism seem secure" even in a rapidly changing international security environment (162).

Whatever the motivation for the American role in the formation of the postwar Western alliance system, it is a fair bet that the values engendered in Western cooperation in security affairs will be maintained in the years ahead, based on the assumption that these values have become internalized in the systems of Western alliance nations. The maintenance of commonly held values becomes easier, as well, as the economies of the Western powers become more interrelated and reliant upon each other for stability and prosperity.

In contrast to integration theory, which posits the ultimate political unification of the cooperating international actors, this theory stops at the point of predicting political integration for the Western alliance countries. Although specialization and trade in security goods promotes interdependence and international reliance, I am skeptical about the prospects of political integration, because the forces of political comparative advantage constrain the degree to which decisionmakers can move beyond the boundaries of national allegiances.[10] International cooperation to serve mutually held values and goals is one thing; shifting constituent allegiances to a broader political entity is quite another. In sum, my view of the future of Western alliance cooperation is generally positive. We now turn to a final point for discussion: the roles for the Western alliance system in the post–Cold War era.

Alliance Problems after the Cold War

The end of the Cold War created a world in which the Western alliance seemingly has no counterpart of enough importance to justify its continued existence. But to the extent that the Western alliance system has over the years broadened beyond the military realm, the elimination of the Soviet bloc threat does not signal the end of the raison d'être of the alliance. Rather, it merely brings other important issues to the fore and emphasizes other aspects of the alliance.

Moreover, to assert that the military threat to Western interests has been eliminated also ignores that other military threats, unrelated to the Soviet bloc, exist in contemporary international relations. Although one can cynically point to Secretary of Defense Richard Cheney's efforts to find a threat for the Defense Department during 1990–91 as evidence of the bureaucratic politics model of national security decisionmaking, one must also recognize that military threats to Western interests do remain. The following list mentions a few of these military threats in showing the roles for the alliance after the Cold War has ended:

Military Roles

- Minimum deterrence in Europe.
- The maintenance of a nuclear force to help deter nuclear proliferation.
- Allied military and financial cooperation for out-of-area or regional conflicts.
- The continued alliance membership by Germany and Japan to alleviate fears of independent military resurgence.

Nonmilitary Roles

- The identification of development assistance needs in the Development Assistance Committee and the G-7 and the promotion of development assistance.
- Monetary and macroeconomic policy coordination and market intervention.

- Third World debt refinancing coordination within the G-7.
- R&D cooperation.
- Cooperation on global environmental problems.
- Conflict resolution.

Even with the continued need for a military component, the economic and political aspects of the alliance will necessarily become more important. This is certainly the argument put forth by Western alliance policymakers (NATO, 1990), but it goes beyond the rhetoric—it is an acknowledgment that the allies have built an international cooperative framework that serves the interests of its members and will serve also the interests of those excluded from the alliance, notably the newly autonomous Eastern European states.[11] Moreover, the demise of the military structure of NATO need not imply the demise of Western cooperation, since NATO is only one part of the Western relationships developed during the postwar era. Western economic summits—since the mid-1970s, recurrent points of high-level allied contact and consultation—will play an important role in Western economic coordination and security. Former Soviet President Gorbachev's request to attend the July 1991 summit was another piece of evidence that pointed to the centrality of these forums in Western affairs.

The key to alliance adaptation in the future is not the formulation of some new grand strategy for the West or the discovery of some new and urgent military threat. Rather, it is simply the maintenance of the momentum built up since the 1960s that has moved away from an American-controlled alliance system to one where the other allies play greater and greater roles in sustaining Western interests. This spirit of cooperation and interreliance not only means that the United States will increasingly need to obtain the consent and cooperation of its "junior" partners to serve its own security interests; it also means that it will need to allow the allies to become senior partners in particular instances. This certainly appears to be what is developing in terms of the Japanese role as world leader in foreign aid.[12]

American policymakers need to recognize the degree to which other alliance nations have internalized American global values. They can place the interests of the United States in the hands of its allies knowing that those interests will be served. The critical question for the future of alliance affairs is whether American leaders will have enough vision to respond to the requirements of international relations in an interdependent world and choose policies, not of retrenchment but, aimed at producing new types of cooperation in a less militarily threatening world.[13]

The time for American paternalism is past; American policymakers must recognize that being first among equals is a better position than being ahead of the pack. The willingness and ability of other allies to assume more of the burdens of Western security affairs is a good thing for the United States. The stress of imperial overstretch, to borrow Paul Kennedy's (1987) term, seen in budget deficits and extensive international military commitments can be eased if American policymakers recognize the richness of the international relationships that have been fostered throughout the postwar period. American policymakers must also discard the tendency to blame allies for problems, such as the twin deficits, that are largely of American making (Bobrow and Kudrle, 1990), if they wish to strengthen and maintain the alliance.

The continued viability of the Western alliance system is not dependent upon finding a new overarching threat that can produce a reason for solidarity. Military and economic threats will continue, although none may be perceived as urgent as the Soviet threat once was. My hope is that, although American leadership was central to the formation and evolution of the postwar alliance, the current generation of policymakers will be able to ease out of that leadership role and into a system of shared responsibilities that can continue to build on the division of labor within the alliance and capitalize on what the other allies have to offer. If American policymakers truly want the most equitable burden-sharing arrangements possible, they must at times allow others to assume the role of alliance leader. Each alliance member has a stake in the continuation of smooth Western relationships, but they also want the status that should go with membership in the Western club.

Appendix A

Alternative Formal Model I: Multiple Public Goods and the Effects of Comparative Advantage

This model is a simple international trade model adapted for use with public goods. It aids in the development of a new economic theory of international cooperation that encompasses all types of allied cooperation and focuses theoretical attention on the effects of the introduction of multiple public goods and variations in national productive efficiency on the alliance security provision process. It accomplished these tasks without the introduction of consultation to the model. In that way, it is an independent adjustment model, where the second alternative model is not.

Formally, this first alternative model comprises two public goods and no private or numeraire good. A numeraire good is a good used to measure the resources allocated to the goods in question and, in particular, the resources allocated to the public good. It measures the amount of each good, public or private, that is produced or consumed within an individual economic system and within the collective, more generally. Conceptually, it is also used to derive prices for public goods, evaluate demand for the goods in terms of real numerical values, and derive tax or toll schemes to help ensure optimal provision of the public good. Most often, the private numeraire good used for analysis is money, thus giving an absolute value to quantities of the public good. In contrast, this model allows derivation of only relative, not absolute, prices for the public goods in question.[1]

This discussion of the model is divided into three cases, which differ according to the relationship between national production advantages and national welfare functions (security policy preferences). In Case 1, each allied nation in the two-nation model prefers a different good and is the more efficient producer of the good that is preferred. In this model, if the United States prefers a mix of security policies tilted toward the use of military security tools rather than other types of security tools, it is also assumed that the United States has a production frontier that makes it the more efficient producer of military goods than of economic or political alliance goods.

Case 1 is the most developed of the three cases for two reasons. (1) Given comparative political advantage and its relationship to both national security preferences and the implied political production constraints on national leadership, a nation preferring a particular type of security strategy will likely possess an advantage in the production of that good within the alliance. National preferences constrain the ability of leaders to produce particular types of security goods. (2) The other two cases can be discussed more easily in relation to Case 1.

In Case 2, a nation possessing a comparative advantage in the production of military goods actually prefers obtaining more economic goods, and vice versa for the other nation in the two-nation world. In Case 3, each nation possesses different comparative advantages, but both nations prefer either more economic goods than military goods or more military than economic goods. This case results in free riding by one nation on the other but also shows that free riding is a collectively efficient outcome.

Case 1: Matched Preferences and Production Advantages

Case 1 depicts a world of public good provision where optimality is possible under decentralized collective decisionmaking. In other words, the Nash, or independent adjustment, equilibrium is an optimal collective outcome, unlike the results normally associated with models of public good provision. Substantively, the model gives one a glimpse of how policy decisions would be made under a form of government where the only concern is provision of public goods and the parochial concerns manifested within a government do not exist because considerations of private goods do not exist. Although this is a wholly unrealistic world and should be viewed primarily as a pedagogical tool, it nonetheless provides a model of alliance behavior that highlights the moves toward optimality that can be made when differences in the productive abilities of nations are accounted for and when consultation among allies is expressly integrated into the model. The following model allows an examination of alliance security provision in a multiple public goods framework and in isolation from nonsecurity considerations.

Figure A.1 displays the geometry of this two-country, two public

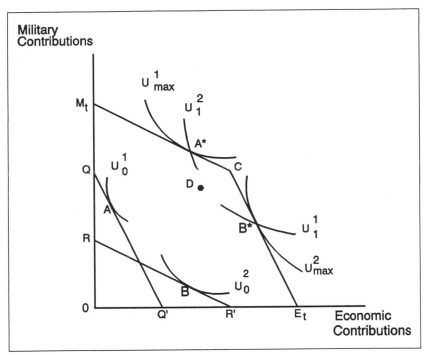

FIGURE A.1   Case 1: Matched preferences and production advantages

goods international trade model. The two countries are Country 1 and Country 2. The two goods are military contributions and economic contributions to the alliance security effort.[2] Military contributions include weaponry, personnel, and basing rights. Economic contributions include not only foreign aid but also contributions to international monetary stabilization and Third World debt relief. Details on types of contributions are given in chapters 5 and 6.

The basic assumptions and components of the model are as follows. First, the production possibility frontiers in the model represent the production trade-offs between military contributions and economic contributions to the alliance for the two countries. The frontier labeled QQ' shows that Country 1 possesses a comparative advantage in the production of military contributions to the alliance. Country 2 has a comparative advantage in the production of economic contributions, as shown by the frontier labeled RR'.

The shape of an individual production frontier is dependent upon both political and economic sources of comparative advantage, as discussed in chapter 3. The indifference curves, U^1_0, U^1_1, U^1_{max}, U^2_0, U^2_1, and U^2_{max}, represent various welfare levels, where welfare can mean any of a variety of abstract concepts and combinations thereof, such as containment, political stability, military deterrence, economic prosperity, and most generally, security. We can assume by the manner in which the respective sets of curves were drawn that Country 1 values military contributions more highly in its utility function than it does economic contributions. In other words, to obtain any given level of security, Country 1 desires more military than economic goods. The converse is assumed true for Country 2.

In isolation from one another or, more specifically, prior to the impetus for alliance formation, Country 1 and Country 2 produce at the points where U^1_0 and U^2_0 are tangent to their respective production functions.[3] Production occurs at point A for Country 1 and at point B for Country 2. When each nation pursues security individually and when these nations have few common interests, A and B represent the points where the greatest individual security can be reached, as defined by the tangent indifference curves.

Once an alliance forms, the production frontier used to determine utility maximization for both nations is no longer the individual production frontier. Because both nations can now consume the production of the other nation, the production frontiers shift outward to form the kinked production frontier shown by endpoints M_t and E_t and midpoint C. This collective frontier, or what Michael Connolly (1972) and Herbert Kiesling (1974) called the consumption possibilities frontier, represents the locus of points for which Country 1 and Country 2's production, taken together, is efficient.[4]

Next, points A^* and B^* represent the "ideal" points for Country 1 and Country 2, respectively. Point A^* is the point where U^1_{max} is tangent to the collective production frontier. The same is true with respect to U^2_{max} and B^*. One way to interpret the substantive meaning of these points is that, if Country 1 were able unilaterally to choose the mix of economic and military goods produced in pursuit of alliance security, the mix would be such that the alliance would produce at point A^*. With similar power held by Country 2, point B^* would be chosen. More likely, neither ideal point will become the collective production point. Note that, as this diagram is drawn, the formation of an alliance and the accompanying pooled production of security relevant goods yield significant gains in welfare for alliance members. In other words, it validates the strength in numbers dictum.

To determine the equilibrium collective production point for this model, the utility maximizing solution for each nation must be derived. To do this, each nation will equate its marginal rate of substitution (the slope of the tangent to its indifference curve) to the slope of the collective production frontier (Kiesling, 1974:408); it will try to obtain its ideal point, which is the point where those values are equal. Given a specific level of production for Country 2, Country 1 will choose to specialize completely in the production of military contributions and produce no economic contributions. Only by specializing totally can Country 1 achieve its highest possible indifference curve. That indifference curve will most likely not be U^1_{max}, because Country 1 could obtain that level of utility only if the given level of Country 2's production (as measured along RR') was in perfect vertical alignment with A^*. Nevertheless, continuing to hold Country 2's production constant, utility maximization by Country 1 would yield a collective production point somewhere on line segment M_tC, an efficient collective production outcome.[5]

In contrast to traditional discussions of public goods provision, there is no incentive in this model for an alliance member to take a free ride on the production efforts of other members of the collective. For instance, taking points A and B as the points where Country 1 and Country 2 produce at the moment of alliance formation, and assuming each nation rationally evaluates its production options, no decision other than total specialization will occur. At alliance inception, the collective production level is shown by point D (the addition and plotting of Country 1's plus Country 2's production of military and economic goods), which is not on the Pareto frontier (the line segment A^*CB^*) nor does it coincide with either nation's ideal point. In this situation, both nations recognize that they can improve their welfare by changing their individual production level. Decreasing production of either good while holding the production of the other good constant will only decrease individual welfare; therefore, each nation decides to specialize in the production of the good for which it holds a comparative advantage. A rational, self-interested evaluation of the costs and benefits of public goods production leads toward optimality rather than away from it, as is the case in the Olson and Zeckhauser model.

When both Country 1 and Country 2 totally specialize in the production of military and economic contributions, respectively, point C is the equilibrium outcome. Once an individual nation chooses to specialize in the production of the good for which it has a comparative advantage, no incentive exists for it to change its production behavior on its own. That nation might wish to move closer to its ideal point but cannot do so unilaterally. If Country 1 tries to improve its situation by decreasing its production of military contributions and not increasing its economic ones (i.e., producing inefficiently with reference to its own production frontier), the collective production point drops directly below point C, thus decreasing welfare for both nations. If Country 1 chooses to produce a mix of the two goods while still producing efficiently, the collective production point remains on the collective production frontier but moves closer to Country 2's ideal point. Although the new production point is efficient, the move to that point is not a Paretian move, because it takes place within the Pareto optimal set. In the first case, both nations lose by Country 1's actions; in the second, Country 1 loses and Country 2 gains. In neither case will Country 1 choose to change its total specialization production point. Similar reasoning follows for Country 2.

Mancur Olson and Richard Zeckhauser (1967, 1970) did suggest that greater efficiency in the provision of public goods could be achieved by specializing along comparative advantage lines. They did not, however, develop this argument to the extent done here and continued to consider alliance security efforts of military relevance alone. Thus, this international trade model indicates how cross-issue burden sharing might develop among allies and, more generally, how burdens might be shared among members of any group dealing with multiple public goods. We now must consider how the "small exploit the large" hypothesis of the Olson and Zeckhauser model fits with the present model.

Case 1A: National Size Discrepancies

In Olson and Zeckhauser's model, the small nations of an alliance do not have an incentive to contribute to the production of the alliance public good because the larger nations value the production of this good more than do the smaller ones. As a result, a large nation will produce the public good for the alliance by itself, regardless of the public good production by the smaller nations. For large nations, the benefits of producing the good on its own outweigh the costs of production, even when other alliance nations free ride on its efforts.

In contrast to this result, size discrepancies in the context of the multiple public goods setting of this model will not necessarily lead to the free-rider behavior hypothesized by Olson and Zeckhauser. Proceeding from the same basic assumptions outlined for figure A.1, figure A.2 displays a two-country international trade model where substantial size differences exist between the two nations. This size differential is shown by the way the production possibilities frontiers are drawn for the two nations. The production frontier for Country 1 remains QQ' and for Country 2 remains RR'. But in contrast to the frontiers drawn in figure A.1, these frontiers do not cross. Rather, Country 1's frontier completely envelops Country 2's frontier, demon-

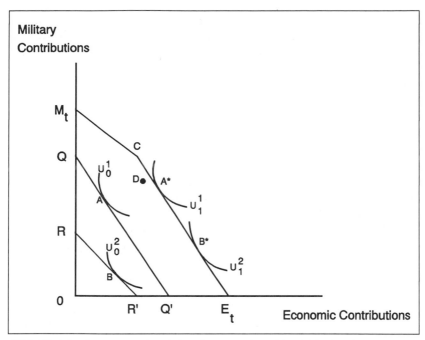

FIGURE A.2   **Case 1a: National size discrepancies with matched preferences and production advantages**

strating that Country 1 is able to produce more of both military and economic goods than Country 2 can produce. In the context of the theory of comparative advantage, however, Country 2 still possesses a comparative advantage in the production of economic goods.

Point *D* is the collective consumption/production point at the moment of alliance formation. Taking the indifference curves as drawn, it is apparent that an outcome similar to that shown in figure A.1 will occur in this instance as well. In other words, there is no general tendency toward suboptimal production of the alliance goods and, more important for the purpose of examining this diagram, there is no general tendency for the small nation to free ride on the production of the larger nation. Each nation confronted with the consumption outcome indicated by point *D* will change its own production levels of the two goods, resulting in optimal collective production of the two goods. The alliance production point will be determined by Country 1, the large nation, as it tries to obtain its ideal point: given total specialization by Country 2, Country 1 will produce that mix of the two goods that moves it closest to its own ideal point. Ultimately, the exact location of the collective production point and the pattern of specialization will depend upon the location of the indifference curves. Even so, free-rider behavior will not necessarily occur in this model.

In contrast to Olson and Zeckhauser's result, and given the assumptions of this model, there is no general incentive for the small to exploit the large. This model suggests that small nations may well make contributions to the alliance effort commensurate to their size and in accordance with the comparative advantages they possess in the production of certain goods.

Although it is too lengthy a subject to address thoroughly here, figures A.1 and A.2 also indicate that appraisals of the future of international cooperation put forth by hegemonic stability theorists (see for instance Gilpin, 1987; Kindleberger, 1973, 1976, 1981, 1986; Keohane, 1984) are needlessly pessimistic. This is because hegemonic stability theory, like past alliance models, focuses on the provision of a single public good. In hegemonic stability theory, the single public good is a liberal international trading system and is provided only when a single dominant economic power exists in the system. But when one considers the provision of security in a multiple public goods setting, there are great incentives for nations to contribute to collective security, whether economic or military, in greater and greater amounts as they grow. In contrast to the predictions of hegemonic stability theory, American relative decline should lead to greater allied cooperation rather than less.

Case 2: Mismatched Preferences and Production Advantages

When national preference functions do not correspond with production advantages, a suboptimal collective outcome will occur, but their is no explicit tendency to free ride. There is no incentive to move toward an efficient collective outcome, as there was in Case 1. This can be understood by examining figure A.3. Figure A.3 differs from figure A.1 in that the nation with a comparative advantage in the production of military contributions (Country 1) prefers a mix of security policies oriented toward economic contributions rather than military contributions (as was the case in figure A.1). The converse mix of advantage and preference is true for Country 2.

Given these preferences and an initial collective production point *D,* there is no incentive for either country to change its production decision and increase its production of either type of good. If Country 1 specialized in producing military contributions, the collective pro-

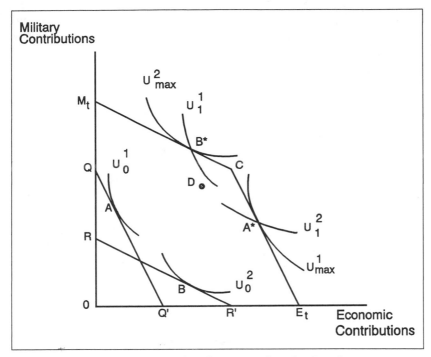

FIGURE A.3   Case 2: Mismatched preferences and production advantages

duction outcome would move farther away from Country 1's ideal point. For identical reasoning regarding its ideal point, Country 2 will not specialize in producing economic contributions.

Moreover, if Country 1 took matters into its own hands and produced more economic goods (even though it is relatively inefficient in doing so), collective production would move toward Country 1's ideal point but the collective outcome would move to a lower welfare frontier. It would also be likely to stimulate Country 2 to increase its production of military goods, decreasing collective welfare even farther.

This has implications for the applicability of Case 1 to the Western alliance and for alliance theory more generally. This case suggests that alliances are unstable and will deteriorate over time when mismatched preferences exist. In this situation, incentives can cause alliance production of public goods to drop even lower than the suboptimal levels in the original alliance formation process (point D). As a result, the strength in numbers security obtained by the allies upon alliance formation will dissipate and, quite possibly, lead to doubts about the efficacy of the collective arrangements.

In contrast, Case 1 demonstrates conditions where allies become dependent upon one another, and little incentive exists to move away from the collectively efficient frontier. This indicates that alliances possessing matched preferences and production advantages are more stable and enduring. With regard to the substantive argument of this book, one could attribute the durability of the Western alliance system to such a preference/production advantage relationship.

Case 2 equates with an outcome of single-play prisoner's dilemma and also with the "liberal paradox."[6] As originally shown by Amartya Sen (1970) and elaborated upon by Nicholas Miller (1977) and John Aldrich (1977), if individuals can choose according to their preferences (liberalism), then Pareto optimal outcomes may not occur depending upon the ordering of those preferences: liberalism and Pareto optimality must be traded off. Case 2 is an instance wherein freedom to choose a security production mix leads to Pareto suboptimality, because of the nature of the mismatched preferences. Only by eliminating liberal choice and coercing allies to specialize counter to their preferences could an optimal outcome be obtained.

Case 3: An Optimal Free-Rider Result

Even when the effects of comparative advantage are accounted for, a free-rider case can emerge in an alliance if all nations prefer the same mix of security goods. For instance, if both nations in figure A.4 prefer a more military-oriented security policy as evidenced by the locations of the points of tangency to their individual production frontiers, the nation possessing an advantage in the production of military goods will bear the lion's share of the alliance military production burden when the alliance forms. To begin, both nations have ideal points on the same section of the collective frontier, and point D again is the initial point of alliance security aggregation. Given these points, Country 1 will seek to move the alliance toward the ideal point by specializing in military production and capitalizing on its production advantage. Country 1's action gets the alliance onto the collective frontier. Country 2 will likely make minor adjustments to its production mix in an effort to move the alliance toward its ideal point.[7] Country 2's major contribution to the alliance effort will be the economic contributions it makes to move the alliance to its ideal point and also its small military contribution.

While this outcome is clearly a free-rider result, it is still a collectively efficient outcome in contrast to the free-rider result of the Olson and Zeckhauser model. This is due to the fact that the numeraire has

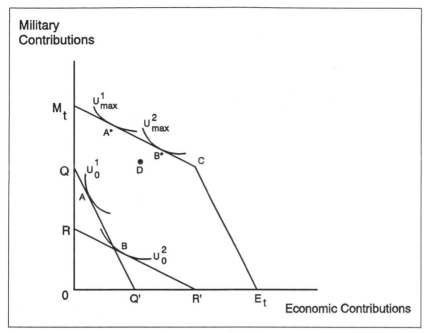

FIGURE A.4   Case 3: An optimal free-rider result

been eliminated from this model. Case 3 also demonstrates that the Olson and Zeckhauser model is a special case in alliance security provision. Their model applies only when allies have the same security policy preferences or, more formally, when only a single public good is desired by the allies. An alliance of purely military importance would fit this case.

Given the different international circumstances that drive alliance formation, free riding might result or it might not depending upon the breadth of the alliance relationships. One can also envision alliance preferences evolving, thus changing the relationship among allies. In the Western alliance case, although the Soviet threat in the immediate post-war period was the driving force behind the formation of NATO and bilateral agreements with Japan, these relationships quickly moved beyond the single military dimension, as the Marshall Plan, recovery aid to Japan, and the OECD and other organizations began to play a greater role in Western relationships. Therefore, although the Western alliance began as a Case 3 alliance, it evolved into a Case 1 alliance. This hypothesis is examined in chapters 4, 5, and 6.

Appendix B

Alternative Formal Model II:
Public Goods, Private Goods, and
Rational Cooperation

The second alternative model of the alliance allocation process is composed of a single public good and a single private good. In contrast to the simple public goods model, considerations of common interest and consultation among alliance members and the possession of varying degrees of efficiency by alliance members are introduced to this model. This addition provides opportunities for gains through trade along comparative advantages lines. The concept of comparative advantage is combined with rational consultation in an effort to examine the effects of their introduction to the public goods model, even when private goods are explicitly factored into the alliance consideration. This model is a substantially reorganized and revised version of a model first presented by Herbert Kiesling (1974) and critiqued by Michael Connolly (1976).

Suboptimal Outcomes after Independent Adjustment

Public goods theory has led analysts to believe that allies have little incentive to contribute to the provision of alliance defense. Two alliance defense outcomes are therefore likely: either it will not be provided to the extent necessary or the smaller nations will free ride on the "benevolence" of the larger nation or nations. This section illustrates this provision problem.

Figure B.1 presents the geometry of the argument. The assumptions of the model are as follows. First, there are two goods: one public and one private. Quantities of the public good are measured on the horizontal axis and are valued positively in both directions from the origin. Quantities of the private good are measured on the vertical

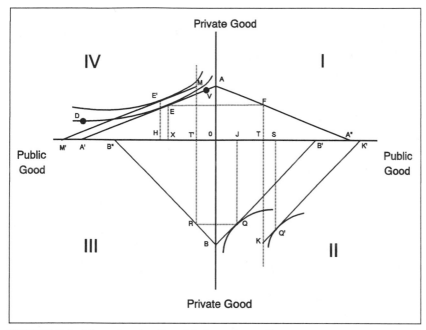

FIGURE B.1   The suboptimality of independent adjustment
Source: Based on Kiesling (1974:408, fig. 3)

axis and are also positive in both directions. In the alliance context, private goods could be nonsecurity consumable goods for an individual nation or side payments made by one alliance nation to another to help finance alliance security costs. The offset payments made by West Germany to the United States to help American balance of payments problems and to pay for the American presence in West Germany is one example. Todd Sandler also pointed to a variety of largely private defense costs. The private portions of foreign aid might also be included here.

Country 1's production frontier is *AA'*. Country 2's production frontier is *BB'*. As drawn, Country 1 can produce the public good more efficiently than one Country 2, but Country 2 can produce the private good more efficiently than can Country 1. The lines *AA"* and *BB"* are the frontiers that show the amount of public good spill-out produced by each nation, following directly from the nonexclusive character of the public good. For example, if Country 1 produces at point *E*, it provides a spill-out of amount *0T* of the public good for Country 2 to consume. The spill-out frontier also measures the perceived shift of a nation's production frontier in response to the spill-in from the other nation.

Before an alliance is formed between Country 1 and Country 2, Country 1 produces at point E, and Country 2 produces at point Q. In other words points E and Q are the points where the individual country's marginal rate of transformation (MRT) equals the marginal rate of substitution (MRS). Once the alliance forms, however, each nation consumes the amount of the public good produced by the other. Country 1 receives $0T'$ of spill-in from Country 2, and its consumption frontier becomes MM'.[1] Country 2 receives $0T$ of spill-in, and its consumption frontier becomes KK'. The outward shift of the frontiers for each nation in turn changes the point of tangency between the nation's indifference curve and the consumption frontier. As a result of these changes, each nation decreases its production of the public good and increases production of the private good. Hence, where both nations were consuming amount $0X + 0J$ of the public good at the moment of alliance formation, they consume the lesser amount $T'H + TS$ of the public good after one round of independent adjustment; after the alliance forms, these nations each produce less of the public good than they did originally. This is the point of analysis where traditional public goods approaches have stopped, thus concluding that alliances will produce suboptimal amounts of alliance defense unless substantial private benefits are produced through individual defense production, as suggested by Bruce Russett and Todd Sandler.[2]

The Possibilities for Intraalliance Trade

Construction of the trading case for public goods must begin with the assumption that both nations have a rational interest in increasing public good production after the independent adjustment outcome of Figure B.1 (Kiesling, 1974:409–10). Since a primary reason for alliance formation is power augmentation and increased security and since neither nation obtains the full benefits of alliance formation after independent adjustment, I assume that some action will be taken to rectify the suboptimal outcome shown in figure B.1. Each seeks increased public goods provision by joining the alliance and now attempts to achieve those levels through negotiated collective production decisions.

The revelation of national production functions must be explicit in these negotiations.[3] The cost curves themselves are functions of political as well as economic factors. Through negotiation and the cost revelation process, alliance members will be able to determine which nation produces what good at the lowest cost. These differences

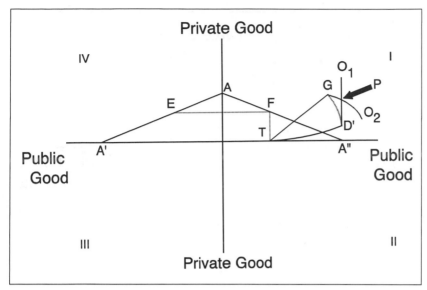

FIGURE B.2 The public goods trading set

in costs become evident once offer curves are derived for the goods in question. Offer curves O_1 and O_2 are shown in figure B.2. Offer curves can provide the basis for decisions regarding increased alliance production efficiency. The boundaries and contents of the three-sided figure TGD' are a set of more efficient public goods production outcomes, which can be obtained through the alliance decisionmaking process. Derivation of this more efficient production set follows.

Offer curves for private goods as discussed in international trade theory are used to show export supply and import demand for a given pair of relative prices. Figure B.3 illustrates the derivation of Country 2's private good offer curve, O_2. The origin of O_2 is located at point T, because this is the point indicating the amount of public good spill-in that Country 2 receives from Country 1. Any negotiation for increased public good production begins from the point that measures the amount of "free" public good Country 2 receives.[4] By construction, every point on the offer curve for private goods is a point where a nation's marginal rate of substitution between the two goods is equal to the trading price. In other words, given any price, the offer curve allows one to determine how much an exporter will supply of the good and how much an importer will demand at that price. For example, Country 2 would supply (offer) amount $0C$ of the private good in exchange for Country 1 increasing production of the public good by amount TV.

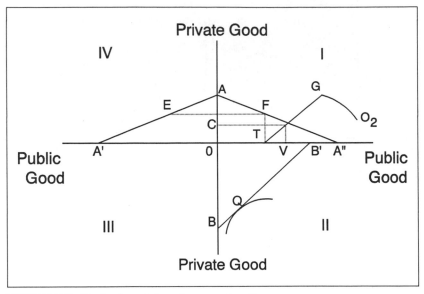

FIGURE B.3 **Derivation of the private goods offer curve**

Production function *BB'* exhibits constant opportunity costs to scale, causing offer curve O_2 to be a straight line. This means that O_2 is infinitely elastic along the segment *TG*. Point *G* is the point where Country 2 is no longer willing to continue offering more and more of the private good for export. The exact location of this point can be determined only through empirical testing. Beyond point *G* the nation is willing to offer less and less of the good for export regardless of the price. In other words, curve O_2 is inelastic beyond point *G*. In addition, when dealing only with private goods and assuming no trade restrictions are imposed by any of the trading parties, the intersection of the importer's offer curve with the exporter's offer curve is a stable optimum equilibrium. It is also the point where relative prices of the two goods in question are the same for each nation.

Offer curves for public goods must be constructed in a somewhat different fashion than those for private goods. Definitionally, an offer curve for public goods shows the amount of the private good that must be paid to the producer by other alliance nations for that producer to produce and consume more of the public good (Kiesling, 1974:409). This derivation is shown in figure B.4. Again, the origin is point *T*, because it represents the public good production that Country 2 receives regardless of any negotiations among allies. Geometrically, one can construct a public good offer curve by plotting the set of points that measures the difference between a nation's cost curve (*AA'*) and

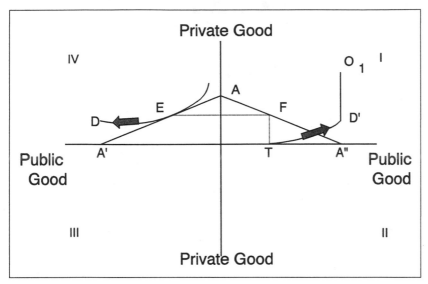

FIGURE B.4 Derivation of the public goods offer curve

its marginal rate of substitution between the public and private goods, as represented by the nation's indifference curve (the tangent at point E). This difference is measured as Country 1 shifts to higher production levels for the public good (i.e., as it moves closer to the public good axis along AA').

The vertical distance measured from point A' (the total public good specialization production point for Country 1) to point D corresponds to the vertical distance from point A'' on the spill-out frontier (AA'') to point D' on curve O_1. The public goods offer curve indicates the minimum payment amount a nation would require for it to increase public goods production to a specific level while remaining on its present indifference curve. For instance, if Country 1 were asked to produce at point A', it would require an amount of the private good equal to the vertical distance $A'D$ (the same distance as $A''D'$) as payment for its increased production. This payment would then satisfy Country 1's minimum private good needs (Kiesling, 1974:410, 415–16).

Because the model presents a case where spill-outs originate in both countries, two sets of offer curves can be derived and both will be subject to examination by alliance members during the cost revelation process. These two sets of curves are displayed in the first and third quadrants of figure B.5. This figure superimposes figure B.1 through B.4 on one another. The set of curves in the first quadrant is Country

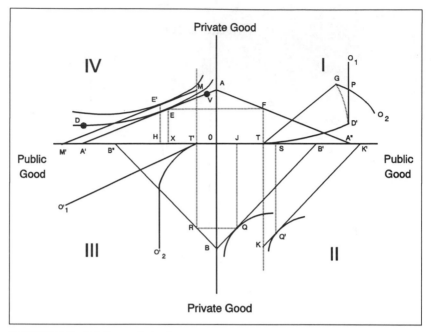

FIGURE B.5 Public goods trade
> *Source:* Based on Kiesling (1974:408, fig. 3). Modification of Kiesling's model made by Connolly (1976) are included in the first quadrant.

1's public good offer curve and Country 2's private good offer curve as derived in figures B.3 and B.4. The set of curves in the third quadrant is Country 1's private goods offer curve and Country 2's public goods offer curve. As is evident from the original production functions, but also as reflected by the slopes of the offer curves, Country 1 can produce the public good at a lower cost than can Country 2. Country 2, on the other hand, has an advantage in the production of the private good. Thus the set of offer curves in the first quadrant will determine the trading outcome. If one uses the set of curves in the third quadrant, no gains are available from trade, as indicated by the divergence of the two curves outward from their origin at point T'.

The space in the first quadrant with corners TGD$'$ is the set of more efficient trade possibilities for the two countries. Moreover, line segment GD' is the locus of optimal points for public goods provision (Connolly, 1976:704). This only proves, however, that it is possible to reach an optimum level of public goods production but not what level of production will actually be decided upon by the two countries.[5] One is not able to determine this outcome specifically, although one can make a number of conjectures about the outcome and say that any outcome within or on the boundaries of TGD' will be closer to optimality than if there were no trading and the original independent adjustment outcomes were left as is. First, implicit in the discussion of the construction of the public goods offer curve is the idea that the offer curve represents the minimum amount that Country 1 would require in payment for increased public goods production. But as Kiesling suggested, if the chosen trading point is on Country 1's offer curve, O_1, then all the gains from trade are obtained by Country 2. This is because, for points on O_1, Country 1 remains on the same indifference curve it started on. Therefore, it is likely that Country 1 will try to obtain a trading point somewhere within the bounds of the offer curves and as close to O_2 as possible.

There is another reason, related to the first, why the exact location of the equilibrium trading point is indeterminate. Because the true shape of the individual indifference curves are not necessarily revealed by the trading nations, Country 1 will likely find it in its interest to skew the location of its offer curve upward by demanding a payment greater than that needed to remain only at its present indifference level.[6] If Country 1 were to do this, both countries would then gain from trade, and public goods provision would increase, although not to an optimal level. If Country 1 did not try to skew its offer curve upward and accepted a bargain on its offer curve, it would remain at its original welfare level, and all the gains from trade would go to Country 2.

Therefore, introducing differences in productive efficiency (economic and political comparative advantages) and consultation among allies to the alliance security provision model demonstrates that provision outcomes closer to optimality than previously hypothesized will be obtained by an alliance. This is true even if negotiations are not entirely cooperative, a condition that occurs even among the closest allies. As a result, this analysis leaves one with a more positive theoretical appraisal of the opportunities for intra-alliance cooperation than much of the alliance literature and adds reasons for increased alliance security provision to those presented by Russett and Sandler.

One final clarification should also be made. Although the model presented above is static, this does not mean that alliance affairs are static as well. Alliance political relationships and strategic needs evolve, producing changes in the indifference and production functions of alliance nations. These changes ultimately affect the nature of the bargains struck by alliance nations in the pursuit collective security. Because national indifference curves are used to construct the offer curves above, changes in preferences also change the boundaries of the possible trading outcomes. The equilibrium outcome decided upon by alliance na-

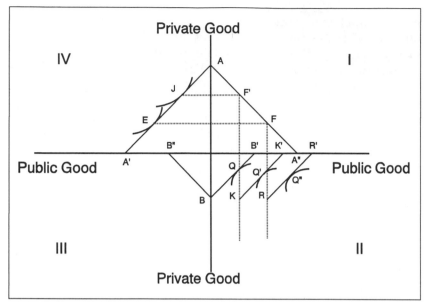

FIGURE B.6   **National size discrepancies and the probability of free riding**
Source: Based on Kiesling (1972:29, fig. 9).

tions is politically determined and is subject to changes in preference functions, which are politically determined within alliance nations.

As a result, one must make a distinction between an equilibrium trading point, as in the model, and political stability. It is possible, given the changeable nature of international political relationships, that an alliance can be politically stable even though it frequently changes the location of its equilibrium public goods trading point. The public goods trading model is a theoretical construct to help define the nature and boundaries of the bargains among alliance members; it does not provide a specific hypothesized outcome for alliance security provision.

A Brief Comment on National Size Discrepancies

The outcome for public goods provision when there are large size differences between alliance nations depends upon the location of the points of tangency between the indifference curves and the production frontier. This is especially true with regard to the positioning of the large nation's initial production point. Figure B.6 displays the geometry of these ideas. Assuming that Country 1 has an advantage in the production of the public good and its frontier is *AA'*, the mix of the two goods chosen for individual consumption will determine the level of spill-out going to Country 2. If Country 1 chooses to produce at point E, Country 2 will receive a large amount of spill-in. If point J is chosen by Country 1, a smaller amount of spill-in will be received by Country 2.

In the first case, discussed by Kiesling (1972:28), the small nation (Country 2) receives so much spill-in that its own production of the public good is reduced to minimal proportions. If trade takes place, "the larger [country] must often trade at the small [country's] preferred price, since the smaller [country] runs out of demand before the larger runs out of supply." In the second case, however, the smaller country's demand for the public good will be higher, providing greater possibilities for trade to occur and greater maneuverability in bargaining for both sides. The equilibrium in the second case ends up being determined by the same factors as when the nations were of similar size.

Notes

Chapter 1 International Western Security and the Theory of Public Goods

1. Throughout this book the Western alliance means the relationships among the United States, Japan, and Western Europe.

2. This of course ignores the possibility that the apple or the aspirin can be cut in two. Still, consumption of part of the apple does not allow additional consumption of that part.

3. National defense is often offered as an example of a public good. It is fully joint because consumption by one citizen does not diminish its availability for other citizens. It is also fully nonexcludable for all who live within the nation's borders. Even if an individual does not pay taxes to provide for the good, and goes to jail, that person is still not excluded from consumption unless the jail is located outside national borders.

4. This notion of free riding is what Marwell and Ames (1979, 1980, 1981) and Alfano and Marwell (1981) call the "strong free-rider" hypothesis. In a strong free-riding situation, none of the public good is provided by the collective through voluntary means. The "weak free-rider" hypothesis states that public goods will be provided by the collective but only at a suboptimal or inefficient level.

5. This type of marginal cost sharing would result in efficient production of the public good as defined by Samuelson (1954). An optimal outcome for public good production requires that the sum of the individuals' marginal rates of substitution equal the marginal rate of transformation for the good.

6. See for instance Ypersele de Strihou (1967), Russett (1970), Starr (1974), Sandler and Cauley (1975), Sandler (1977), Sandler and Forbes (1980), Sandler, Cauley, and Forbes (1980), Murdoch and Sandler (1982: 1984), and Nelson and Lepgold (1986). The work of Sandler and his associates, particularly, built on theoretical studies in the areas of public choice and the theory of clubs. The pure public good assumption and the associated literature are discussed more fully in chapter 2.

7. Eisenhower's pressure on French and British currencies during the

1956 Suez crisis and Reagan's technology transfer restrictions in 1982 regarding the Siberian natural gas pipeline controversy are only two examples that illustrate American willingness to pressure the allies.

8. The Nunn Amendment (*Congressional Record,* 1984) is one of the few instances of congressional action in this area. If it had passed, it would have mandated that U.S. troops be gradually withdrawn from Western Europe beginning at the end of 1987, if Western European defense expenditures did not meet the 3 percent real growth figure agreed to by the alliance.

9. See for instance Krause's (1968) discussion of the incentives for American support of the formation of the European Community and British membership therein. He suggests that one reason that the United States was willing to support the formation of the EC was that a common market was perceived as a way of promoting stronger economic growth in Europe, thus providing a rationale for the assumption of greater defense burdens by the Europeans.

Chapter 2 Alliance Defense and Collective Action

1. See for instance the mention in Sandler and Forbes (1980:429) of the foreign exchange implications of overseas basing and of the domestic industrial implications of military defense.

2. The term *spill-in* was first used in the alliance context by Sandler and Cauley (1975).

3. See for instance Bobrow (1990), which focuses not on the standard guns-butter trade-off but on the way Japan "satifices" across policy areas to meet its domestic and international policy goals.

4. The figure of $281 billion was the FY 1993 defense budget proposed by President Bush in his 1992 State of the Union address.

5. In this case, Little Atlantis's *MRS* is measured as the slope of its evaluation curve as it approaches the origin (point 0) in the limit.

6. Olson and Zeckhauser also examined foreign aid donations and found additional support for their model with this data. Using three slightly different data types, they obtained correlations of GNP to percentage of GNP spent on aid ranging from .439 to .770 (1966:276). But as is shown in chapter 5, the relationship between foreign aid and GNP has changed drastically since their study. In addition, although they examined both alliance military expenditures and foreign aid donations, this was not done in the context of a multiple public goods framework. In other words, they treated foreign aid and defense spending as discrete categories for analysis.

7. Sandler and his associates in a number of general theoretical pieces focused on this third assumption: the possibility that consultation in some form does take place. This work is discussed in chapter 3.

8. The concept of congestion as it applies to public goods is related to the concept of carrying capacity as it is used in demography and ecological studies and also as it relates to the tragedy of the commons.

9. If preservation of peace is the alliance's public good, the American nuclear umbrella would not be the means for achieving that good. Rather, the combined forces of the United States and the U.S.S.R. created the balance of terror and ultimately preserved the peace. As nuclear arms talks demonstrate,

the nations of the world place great value on a balance between the superpowers' arsenals and not on a monopoly by one or the other power.

10. Joe Oppenheimer pointed out that Sandler's analysis ignores the private benefits resulting from the production of nuclear weaponry, such as research and development programs and the technological spin-offs they produce.

11. Tactical nuclear warfighting strategies are often not considered protective. As one reviewer noted, most official justifications for warfighting strategies are made in terms of deterrence rather than defense or denial. This example, however, is used as a further illustration of the ambiguity of the protective/deterrent classification scheme.

Chapter 3 Why Nations Cooperate

1. An increased knowledge base approaches a pure public good, while contributions directly related to Western security and not available for world consumption are public goods only for the Western club. Sales of technology also will at times be a private good that can be used as side payments for other alliance security goods.

2. A Pareto optimal situation is a situation where one individual in a collective cannot be made better off without making someone else worse off.

3. Public good offer curves were first developed by Connolly (1972). An offer curve is by definition the locus of points showing the amount of a good that will be offered for export by a nation at a given price. It also shows the amount that will be desired for import by other nations at the same price.

4. For instance, for a country like the United States, which prefers military security strategies, preferred alliance policies for dealing with Third World instability might center upon arms sales and upon enhancing the stability of pro-Western, even if nondemocratic, regimes. For Japan, it might mean policies focusing on the economic roots of Third World instability.

5. Side payments are monetary payments made from one nation to another nation when the second nation is providing a public good for both nations. One example in the postwar security system are the offset payments made by West Germany to the United States to defray the costs of stationing troops on German soil for military defense purposes. See Sloan (1985a) for a thorough discussion of these payments and the agreements that established them as a part of alliance security arrangements.

6. The constraints on a decisionmaker's ability to conduct international affairs created by domestic political forces parallel the ideas of Putnam (1988). In that study, Putnam identified the complexity of international cooperation resulting from the fact that political games are played at both domestic and international levels.

7. For instance, the Japanese defense industry at times has problems regarding economies of scale because of the size of its armed forces and, more important, because of the Japanese ban on weapons exports. As a result, Japan must at times purchase weapons from abroad that it would produce domestically, if it could generate economies of scale.

8. In nonspecialized production, each alliance nation contributes the same

percentage of GNP to the production of a particular alliance public good. In other words, all nations might spend 5 percent of GNP on the military and 0.4 percent of GNP on foreign aid.

9. Sandler and Forbes (1980:432–33) stated that, because NATO does little in the way of commonly financed military projects, it is a loosely integrated alliance structure. But security provision goes beyond the military arena: policy coordination occurs within the alliance because of Western political and economic interdependence.

10. In a comment on Kiesling's 1974 article, Connolly (1976) stated that what Kiesling showed to be the optimal point for public good provision is actually a point where overproduction of the public good occurs. Nonetheless, Connolly's point is essentially a technical one and does not negate the conclusion that trade will increase public good production and efficiency.

11. Hardin (1982) has shown that the problems of public good provision are equivalent to the situation engendered by an n-person prisoner's dilemma game.

12. Axelrod's theoretical and empirical findings on the positive effects of repeated play (or iteration) in inducing cooperative outcomes in prisoner's dilemma games fit closely with earlier theoretical findings by Luce and Raiffa (1957:97–102), Taylor (1976:105), and others.

13. See appendix B for a formal model of public good provision incorporating ideas of consultation with the implications of comparative advantage. The model provides a clear proof of Borcherding's assertion.

14. This discussion of obligation or a sense of peer pressure benefits from the ideas contained in Klosko (1990) and from personal discussions with Davis Bobrow.

15. Oneal (1990b) defined higher levels of cooperation as a weak correlation between economic size and military burden.

16. Oneal (1990b) went beyond military expenditures but lumped foreign aid and military spending into a single measure of alliance contribution. The implications of this methodological choice for evaluations of alliance security are discussed in chapter 5.

17. The appendixes show that the free-rider problem is a special case of the public goods allocation process. The free-rider result is contingent upon national preferences regarding security policy tools. Generally, this result occurs when nations have single-dimensional security preferences. For example, if both large and small nations prefer a military security strategy, then free riding will likely take the form of the smaller nations consuming the military public good production of the larger nation. But if preferences do not match, then security policy specialization will likely exist, even with size differences among alliance nations.

Chapter 4 Political Comparative Advantage

1. See Bobrow (1984) and Japanese Defense Agency (1987) for discussions of Japanese definitions of security. Schmidt (1978), Flynn et al. (1981), Sloan (1985a, 1985b), and Flynn and Rattinger (1985) all present ideas regarding the redefinition of national security by various NATO countries.

2. The data in the Martilla study show that in 1988 the American public

was more concerned about threats to security posed by international drug trafficking, terrorism, and nuclear proliferation in the Third World than it was about the threat of Soviet expansionism (265–67).

3. The security utility function is the curve that illustrates the combination of security goods desired by alliance nations and the collective more generally. See appendixes.

4. See Almond (1950) and Converse (1964) on the instability of public attitudes toward foreign policy issues. In the public choice literature, Arrow (1951) and numerous others have pointed to the potential for cyclical and unstable outcomes in majority rule settings and the logrolling and vote trading associated with these outcomes.

5. Cyclical outcomes refer to the potential for vote trading and logrolling in majority rule decision-making situations, making it difficult for a stable (and lasting) decision to be achieved under majority rule.

6. At the very least, one can point to the public's role in the policy process in liberal democracies as one of agenda setting (Marsh and Fraser, 1989:12–14). Payne (1990) and Putnam (1988) point to the constraining effects of domestic politics and public opinion on the international decisions made by national leaders.

7. The threat-of-war results are also supported by surveys of the Group of Five (United States, United Kingdom, France, Japan and West Germany). These data show 54 percent of Americans answering that war was either very or somewhat likely in the following fifteen years; 35 percent of Japanese, 29 percent of French, 25 percent of British, and 16 percent of West German respondents chose one of those categories. Except for Japan and France, the rank ordering of these percentage figures is the same as that in table 4.3 for the threat-of-war category (Hastings and Hastings, 1987:592; survey by Gallup International Research Institute). Tracking allied nation attitudes on the risk of war from 1971 to 1989 produced similar findings (Gallup Political Index, various years).

8. About this same period of time (when the most hostile anti-Soviet rhetoric was issuing from the Reagan administration), survey data found that the United States was perceived by European publics as just as great a threat to peace as was the Soviet Union (Gallup Political Index, 1982).

9. In 1987, for instance, only the United States and Greece among alliance members spent more on defense as a percentage of GDP than did Great Britain (Cheney, 1989:96).

10. In 1978 NATO decided that each alliance nation should increase defense spending by an average of 3 percent above inflation each year over a five-year period (Sloan, 1987:80), but few nations met this goal. The non-U.S. NATO average (ranging from 0.2 percent to 3.0 percent during the 1981–86 period) hit this mark only in 1981. The United States, however, exceeded the goal throughout the period, ranging from 4.6 percent to 7.9 percent during the 1981–86 period (Carlucci, 1988:53).

11. Of the fifteen budget categories listed in the General Social Survey used for table 4.6, foreign aid ranked by far the lowest. The categories were space exploration, the environment, health, big cities, crime, drug addiction, education, the condition of blacks, welfare, highways and bridges, Social Security, mass transportation, parks and recreation, the military, and foreign aid.

12. These interviews were conducted under the auspices of the Young

Leaders trip to Japan, 19 October to 30 October 1991. Meetings were held with Japanese officials in the ministries of Foreign Affairs, International Trade and Industry, and the Japanese Defense Agency; with individuals from the private sector side of the defense industry (e.g., Keidanren's Defense Production Committee and Mitsubishi Heavy Industries); and also with elected officials from the Liberal Democratic and Komeito parties.

13. The surveys cited were sponsored by the Atlantic Institute and coordinated by Louis Harris, France.

14. Some would even argue that the American role was as an enforcer of free trade, even if a benevolent enforcer. There is a large body of literature on the role of the United States in the building and maintenance of the liberal trading system and what its relative decline means for the future of this system. See Gowa (1989), Snidal (1985), Keohane (1984), and Lake (1983) for critiques and reviews of the hegemonic stability literature.

15. When asked how to correct the trade imbalance with Japan, American respondents overwhelmingly chose "allowing more US goods abroad and more foreign goods into the US" rather than "restricting imports to the US." Seventy-five percent favored the former option in 1985 and 67 percent in 1983 (Harris Survey, 1985:3). In addition, in a Gallup survey of both opinion leaders and the general population, respondents strongly favored "finding ways for US industry to be more efficient" and "reducing the budget deficit" as better ways than protectionist policies to deal with trade problems with Western Europe (Gallup Organization, 1988).

Chapter 5 Measuring Security Cooperation

1. Oneal (1990b) is the only study to include other expenditures for analysis, but it is based on the flawed empirical assumption that these expenditures can and should be lumped together into a single expenditure category. Olson and Zeckhauser (1966) and Ypersele de Strihou (1967) also examined foreign aid in their analysis of burden sharing. These results are discussed in this chapter.

2. Official development assistance is classified as financial flows "administered with the promotion of economic development and welfare of developing countries as its main objective" and "is concessional in character," that is, an outright grant element is part of the flow (OECD, 1985:280).

3. This argument was put forth by Efigenia Martinez (an opposition party member of the Mexican parliament) at the Conference of MacArthur Foundation Fellows in International Peace and Security, 9–13 January 1988, in Morelos, Mexico. Her central point was that, while the G-7 negotiations are perceived by the North as an example of successful international cooperation in recent years, these negotiations ignore and exclude the economic input and interests of the South. As a result, they do not adequately address contemporary international economic problems.

4. Political public goods are also produced whenever allies take political stands that enhance alliance security. Political stands are often taken at substantial political cost to a nation and should therefore be interpreted as burdens borne for alliance security. The goods produced by such stands are joint in

two ways. First, the degree of jointness depends upon the convergence of general alliance political goals. If allied feelings about a particular issue are similar, then an ally's stand in the face of nonalliance political pressure is a public good. Second, political contributions also produce an externality that one might call the facilitation of cooperation among alliance members. In other words, political forbearance spills over into other alliance issue areas and facilitate cooperation. Through political contributions, a nation builds its political capital within the alliance, providing yet another item regarding alliance security to be negotiated and traded.

5. A nonparametric measure of association was chosen for the first portion of the analysis because of the small number of observations for each year and, more important, because I have no reason to assume that the distribution of the data for such a small population approximates a normal distribution. As Siegel stated, parametric statistics assume that the distribution of the data has the specific shape of the normal distribution. By contrast, nonparametric, or distribution-free, techniques yield conclusions about the data that require fewer qualifications (1956:2–3). The time series for research and development spending is slightly shorter and varies in cross-national completeness depending on the years in question.

6. Please refer to note 12, chapter 4, and the relevant text for further discussion along these lines, particularly as this conceptual issue is perceived by some Japanese officials.

7. This was also the method chosen by Russett (1970) and Sandler and Murdoch (1990) in their analyses of alliance burden-sharing. Significance tests of the Spearman correlations are not used for a number of reasons. By definition, tests of significance are used for making decisions between competing hypotheses about the characteristics of a population based on knowledge obtained from a sample of that population (Morrison and Henkel, 1970:183–84). Significance tests are only legitimately used, however, if the sample data used for testing are a probability sample from the specified population (186). Any other use, including making judgments on data from an entire population, is inappropriate (189–90). The analysis of the present study comes under this last heading, as the countries contained in the analysis compose the relevant population for the study. Additionally, in the instance where not all Western countries are included in the analysis because of data availability, the countries that are included cannot be considered a probability sample. Thus significance tests of the Spearman rank-order correlations are inappropriate in this analysis.

8. For 1960 data, Olson and Zeckhauser obtained a correlation of .582 between national income and the infrastructure military expenditure ratio they created. Using their data (1966:277) but my methodology, the correlation is .521. And using my data and methodology, the correlation is .455. As this shows, the results are similar, regardless of the methodology or data used. For these reasons, the following analysis correlates GDP with GDP shares on each dimension. In addition, the slight differences in the results can as easily be attributed to differences in data as differences in methodology. As two correlations for 1964 show, the data in this analysis yield a correlation of .411, and Olson and Zeckhauser's data yield a correlation of .490. For both data sets, GDP/GNP was correlated with military expenditure as a share of GDP/

GNP. This result for 1964 was seen by Olson and Zeckhauser as support for their hypothesis that larger alliance nations bear disproportionate burdens.

9. Foreign aid donation data were not collected for Spain, Portugal, Greece, or Turkey because their per capita GDP places them in the category of developing countries. Thus these nations are excluded from cross-national aid data, such as those published under the auspices of the Development Assistance Committee (DAC) of the OECD. As a result, overseas development aid figures for the other alliance nations may well include aid to these four countries.

10. Off-the-record interview, Tokyo, 28 October 1991.

11. Katzenstein (1978:20–21) states that of the six largest Western alliance nations (the United States, the United Kingdom, West Germany, Italy, France, and Japan), Japan exhibits the most tightly integrated relationship between the public and private sector.

12. The additional 4 percent of American funding is provided by what UNESCO terms "other funds," or funds that cannot be classified under any other heading (government, private, or foreign).

Chapter 6 International Monetary Cooperation

1. For instance, the IMF's *International Financial Statistics* lists a nation's international currency purchases but does not break those purchases down by currency. In other words, values are aggregates denoted in dollars or special drawing rights.

2. Simply put, the Triffin paradox was that, as the United States continued to run a balance of payments deficit, a point should be reached where the dollar would be so weakened that the deficit would ultimately rectify itself as American goods became cheaper on international markets and more American goods were sold. The paradox, however, arose because the dollar was the centerpiece of the fixed exchange rate system and because the dollar would continue to be in high demand on international markets, even though apparently weakened by the deficit (Calleo, 1982:51). DeGaulle's criticism stemmed from the idea that, through the balance of payments deficit and the preeminent American monetary role, the American economy was allowed to continue expanding at an unrestrained pace without requiring domestic economic adjustment to account for the balance of payments problems. This criticism was especially significant given that the fundamentals of the Bretton Woods economic system assumed that nations would use domestic policies to keep their external accounts in relative long-term balance. Eliminating the American dollar would also produce a shortage of international liquidity and, ultimately, a world recession.

3. It was not until 1960 that the IMF annual report and the *Economic Report of the President* began characterizing the persistent American balance of payments deficit as a "problem" (Solomon 1982:27).

4. I borrow the use of this term in the international monetary realm from Emminger (1977:11). A number of other authors also refer to such burdens in their writings. See for instance, Solomon (1982), Funabashi (1989), and Calleo (1982).

5. The Group of Ten consisted of the United States, Great Britain, Germany, France, Italy, Japan, Canada, the Netherlands, Belgium, and Sweden. IMF members ratified floating rates but were to try to maintain orderly markets.

6. See Williamson (1977) for a thorough account of the reform efforts of the Committee of Twenty.

7. The BIS annual discontinued its coverage of efforts aimed at world monetary reform with its 1975–76 report.

8. After some reluctance and a dispute with the United States, France agreed to a new IMF Article IV that allowed countries to follow any exchange rate practice as long as it was broadly in line with "good monetary citizenship." The only requirement was that states were to cooperate with the IMF in market intervention and in policies aimed to promote orderly economic growth (Odell, 1982:329).

9. In addition to the actions mentioned, other notable interventions also took place and are listed in table 6.1. In particular, Japan, West Germany, and Switzerland intervened in March and April 1979 to maintain their own currencies relative to an appreciating dollar. And in 1980, these same countries relaxed restrictions on capital inflows, thus easing demand for their currencies (BIS, 1978–79:137; 1980–81:125).

10. Kudrle and Bobrow (1991) speculated that cooperation among the G-7 would continue because it serves each country's self-interest. The G-7 countries recognize that prosperity and security are "vitally enhanced through cooperation" (165).

11. Dobson (1991:127) asserted that the United States is not as easily pressured for fiscal policy changes as other governments are and that other governments have even refrained from attempting such pressure because of doubts about its impact.

Chapter 7 The Future of the Western Alliance System

1. These critiques of the alliance's future prospects are at least implicitly based on traditional realist assumptions about the reasons for alliance formation. In particular, see Waltz (1979) and Walt (1987) for theoretical discussions of balance of threat rationales of alliance formation.

2. Economic security concerns were also part of alliance considerations early in the postwar period. The quotations from Cordell Hull and William Clayton earlier in this book point out that American policymakers saw economic security as central to Western interests. For further examination of economic security interests in the early postwar period see, for instance, Pollard (1985) and Holm-Pedersen (1990).

3. For instance, Hahn and Pfaltzgraff (1979); Freedman (1983); Betts (1989); Theis (1989); and Sherwood (1990).

4. One Japanese official remarked that the term *burden sharing* was a "bad word" to the Japanese. He rather preferred the term *responsibility sharing*, as it tends to focus on a more positive set of relationships and also away from the military realm, where the term is usually applied. Off-the-record interview, October 1991, Tokyo.

5. One need only recall the oil dumping in the Persian Gulf and the subsequent well fires to understand the centrality of environmental problems: Saddam Hussein's oil dumping threatened Saudi desalinization plants and the Gulf ecosystem. The fires polluted the air and also damaged the potential for Kuwaiti economic recovery.

6. Deficit financing in the form of inflowing foreign investment, while yielding substantial privately consumed benefits to the United States, also produces a public externality for the alliance, which could be called economic stability or, depending on the amount of economic feedback within the system, even alliancewide economic growth.

7. At a conceptual level, political comparative advantage has significant implications for the free-rider hypothesis. In particular, if one talks about the costs (political and economic) that a nation perceives when making a decision about its alliance contributions, then the free-rider hypothesis may become transparent even on a single dimension. For instance, the Japanese desire to keep its national military expenditures below 1 percent of GDP was perceived as security enhancing, since low Japanese military expenditures kept the Soviets and other Asian nations focused on the United States and not on Japan in terms of the origin of national security threats. Thus what appears to be free riding on the military dimension has really been a calculated evaluation of the level of military expenditure that yielded the highest level of security for the Japanese. I owe this point to Davis Bobrow and Stuart Thorson.

8. Italy may well be making large contributions to the alliance in areas not examined in this study.

9. Calleo's (1987) devolutionary strategy would have had similar effects on alliance solidarity by forcing the Europeans to provide for much more of their own defense needs even before the decline of Cold War tensions. The devolutionary approach was aimed at solving the problem of the American fiscal deficit by pulling most American troops out of Europe and Europeanizing NATO defense. American troop withdrawal would have helped the United States realign its policy instruments with its policy goals and eliminate the fiscal stress (109–10, 126, 215). It would also have demanded significantly larger European military forces. Western alliance proposals for military realignment in the post–Cold War environment need not require substantial European force increases.

10. As Putnam (1988) stated, international cooperation is a two-level game, wherein international strategic concerns must be balanced with the domestic political forces that constrain a decisionmaker's maneuvering room. In other words, given the domestic aspects of two-level negotiations, relinquishing sovereignty and the general subordination of national concerns is problematic.

11. It is unclear what sort of military relationship will ultimately be established in Europe, particularly among non-NATO countries. At this writing, NATO has been reluctant to extend membership to the former Soviet bloc nations, although President Bush has said this may be necessary. Another possibility would be expansion of the Conference on Security and Cooperation in Europe to provide a broad-based security structure with NATO as its core, at least at the start. This has been suggested as NATO's only avenue for future viability by Sloan (1990). If nothing else, NATO has tried to offer political

assurance to the newly autonomous states and has provided for increasing cooperation on scientific and environmental projects and on plans for industrial conversion from military to civilian purposes (Friedman, 1991).

12. The imperative for American decisionmakers to work with the allies was identified by Strange (1990:271).

13. This argument parallel's Nye's (1990:260–61) regarding the inevitability and necessity of American leadership in the future.

Appendix A Alternative Formal Model I

1. The elimination of the numeraire from the analysis has significant methodological and substantive implications. First, it raises serious questions regarding the suboptimality theorem from public goods theory. But although decisions about alliance security provision will necessarily take on a somewhat different form when the numeraire is included in the model, the substantive conclusions regarding specialization in the production of alliance public goods along comparative advantage lines remain the same.

Second, inclusion of the numeraire in an analysis of multidimensional security cooperation implies that monetary values can be compared across the various alliance contribution dimensions. But although the security values (and therefore the monetary values) of these contributions might be equivalent, this is not necessarily true, and any attempt to equate the values is ultimately based on subjective judgments. In essence, only relative comparisons of individual national contributions to alliance security can be made across dimensions. As Buchanan suggests, in "the world without a numeraire," exchange takes on the form of a barter system, where the goods are "priced" by virtue of how much of another good they are worth (1968:123).

2. For both types of contributions (military and economic), the hypothesized specialization behavior would also be hypothesized when the overarching categories of alliance contributions are broken down to their component parts. Thus instead of observing production specialization only across the two categories, it should be observed across the subcategories as well.

3. Past work in the theory of alliances has neglected the impetus for alliance formation. This neglect, in turn, causes some conceptual problems regarding the excludability of alliance security spillovers in terms of what goods are consumed before and after alliance formation. Most likely, the goods produced by an alliance are transformed at the point of alliance formation from largely private to largely public goods. The same can be said for foreign aid. If all goods could be consumed before alliance formation (i.e., without becoming more public), there would be little reason for alliances to form. In some respects, one could interpret alliance formation as a point where security goods become much more public than they were prior to formation.

4. The collective frontier is constructed by assuming that Country 1 is producing amount $0Q$ of military goods (total specialization in military goods) and then plotting the collective frontier as measured by the sum of the two nations' military production and the sum of the two nations' economic production. Essentially, this means displacing RR' vertically by amount $0Q$. For the

half of the collective frontier southeast of point C, total specialization in economic goods is assumed for Country 2, and QQ' is displaced horizontally by amount $0R'$.

5. A disclaimer should be made about the total specialization outcome hypothesized by the model. This result would not occur in reality for both theoretical and political reasons but occurs here because the production frontiers are drawn to show constant opportunity costs to scale. If they were, instead, drawn as smooth curves, indicating increasing opportunity costs, specialization in each nation would occur only to the point where the relative costs of production in each were equal. Politically, specialization will also be limited because each nation will hedge against alliance disintegration so as not to open itself to massive weakness in case of disintegration and because each nation receives some private benefits from the production of each type of good. In this vein, nations will likely produce some of each good because of domestic political demands.

6. I am indebted to Joe Oppenheimer for pointing out the parallel between the situation in Case 2 and these other portions of the public choice literature. The discussion of both Case 2 and Case 3 benefited greatly from a brief, but intellectually intense, discussion I had with Professor Oppenheimer in October 1990. For that and other tutoring sessions, I am most thankful to him.

7. An alternative way that the ideal point could be reached would be for both allies to adjust their mixes of policies (i.e., short of total specialization by Country 1) so that the alliance could move from point D. Whether this method is chosen does little to change the reality that Country 1 will bear a larger military burden than its ally, Country 2.

Appendix B Alternative Formal Model II

1. The term *consumption frontier* was coined by Connolly (1972) to indicate that this frontier is now the one being used by a nation to make consumption decisions. Although the shape of the nation's production frontier remains the same, the public good spill-in that the nation receives allows it to consume as if its production frontier has shifted outward (i.e., as if the nation received an increase in income and is able to reach a higher indifference curve).

2. An outcome wherein some amount of the public good is still produced after independent adjustment, such as in figure B.1, is what Marwell and Ames (1979, 1980, 1981) and Alfano and Marwell (1981) call the "weak free-rider" outcome. In a "strong free-rider" outcome, no public goods at all will be produced by a collective after independent adjustment.

3. This is not to suggest that preference revelation will be perfect or complete. One should assume, however, that if alliances are at least partially cooperative, some revelation of national preferences will occur. As is discussed further on, lying about these preferences may well occur, but efficiency gains can still be made. Lying, ultimately, has an impact on the exact bargain struck between alliance members within the solution set discussed below.

4. Kiesling (1974) and Connolly (1976) disagree on whether point T or point O should be the origin of the trading set. I continue to use Kiesling's location of point T, because this assumes some recognition by the countries

involved that there is a public goods suboptimality problem and action needs to be taken to improve the alliance production outcome.

5. The curved line *GD'* is the locus of tangencies of the two countries' trade indifference curves. The indifference curves are derived relative to each country's offer curve. Point *P* is a point where the public good is being overproduced.

6. The following diverges from Kiesling's analysis because of an analytical error found in his article. He suggested that an individual could pretend his preferences were such that the indifference curve was tangent to a point such as point *V* in figure B.1. He stated that this would then shift the offer curve to the left, making it "above" the real offer curve at all points. While this is correct geometrically, problems arise when considering the original adjustment pattern of the two countries. To assume that Country 1 could use point *V* as its consumption-production point and get away with it implies that Country 2 is unable to measure the spill-in it receives from Country 1 once the alliance forms. Such an assumption is counter to the basic tenets of public goods theory. As a result, my analysis suggests that if lying occurs, it will take the form of misrepresentation of the shape of the indifference curve rather than misrepresentation of the point of tangency. More specifically, Country 1 could pretend that its indifference curve became asymptotic horizontally at a higher level of private goods provision than it actually does. It thus still assumes that Country 2 can accurately gauge the amount of spill-in it receives.

References

ABC News/Washington Post. 1989. Poll. Storrs, Conn.: Roper Center Archives.

Adams, Gordon, and Eric Munz. 1988. *Fair Shares: Bearing the Burden of the NATO Alliance*. Washington, D.C.: Defense Budget Project, Center on Budget and Policy Priorities.

Aldrich, John. 1977. "Liberal Games: Further Comments on Social Choice and Game Theory." *Public Choice* 30:29–34.

Alfano, G., and Marwell, Gerald. 1981. "Experiments on the Provision of Public Goods III: Non-divisibility and Free Riding in 'Real' Groups." *Social Psychology Quarterly* 43:300–9.

Allison, Graham T. 1971. *Essence of Decision: Explaining the Cuban Missile Crisis.* Boston: Little, Brown.

Almond, Gabriel A. 1950. *The American People and Foreign Policy.* New York: Harcourt, Brace.

Arrow, Kenneth J. 1951, rev. ed. 1963. *Social Choice and Individual Values.* New York: John Wiley and Sons.

Auerbach, Stuart. 1990. "CoCom Considered as Arms-Sales Curb," *Washington Post,* 2 August.

Axelrod, Robert. 1984. *The Evolution of Cooperation.* New York: Basic Books.

Axelrod, Robert, and Robert O. Keohane. 1986. "Achieving Cooperation under Anarchy: Strategies and Institutions." In *Cooperation under Anarchy,* edited by Kenneth A. Oye. Princeton: Princeton University Press.

Barry, Brian, and Russell Hardin, eds. 1982. *Rational Man and Irrational Society? An Introduction and Sourcebook.* Beverly Hills: Sage.

Bergsten, C. Fred. 1975. *Dilemmas of the Dollar: The Economics and Politics of United States International Monetary Policy.* New York: New York University Press.

Betts, Richard K. 1989. "NATO's Mid-Life Crisis." *Foreign Affairs.* 68:37–52.

BIS (Bank for International Settlements). Various years. *Annual Report.* Basle: Bank for International Settlements.

Bobrow, Davis B. 1984. "Playing for Safety: Japan's Security Practices." *Japan Quarterly* 31:33–43.

———. 1990. "Eating Your Cake and Having It Too: The Japanese Case."

Paper presented at the annual meetings of the International Studies Association, 10–14 April, Washington, D.C.

Bobrow, Davis B., and Mark A. Boyer. 1985. "Priming the Pump: Japan's Use of the Foreign Aid Instrument." Paper presented at the annual meetings of the International Studies Association, 25–29 March, Anaheim, Calif.

Bobrow, Davis B., and Robert T. Kudrle. 1990. "U.S. Policy and Japan: Beyond Self-Indulgence." *Comparative Strategy* 9:101–15.

Bohm, P. 1972. "Estimating Demand for Public Goods: An Experiment." *European Economic Review* 3:111–30.

Borcherding, Thomas E. 1981. "Comment: The Demand for Military Expenditures: An International Comparison." *Public Choice* 37:33–39.

Boyer, Mark A. 1989. "Trading Public Goods in the Western Alliance System." *Journal of Conflict Resolution* 33:700–27.

———. 1990. "A Simple and Untraditional Analysis of Western Alliance Burden-Sharing." *Defence Economics* 1:243–59.

Breton, Albert. 1970. "Public Goods and the Stability of Federalism." *Kyklos* 23:882–902.

Brown, Harold. 1982. "Challenges Confronting the National Security." Speech before the World Affairs Council, 29 July 1977, San Francisco. In *American Foreign Policy: Basic Documents, 1977–1981*. Washington, D.C.: Department of State.

Brown, Lester, 1977. *Redefining National Security*. Worldwatch Paper 14. Washington, D.C.: Worldwatch Institute.

Buchanan, James M. 1968. *The Demand and Supply of Public Goods*. Chicago: Rand McNally.

Calleo, David P. 1982. *The Imperious Economy*. Cambridge: Harvard University Press.

———. 1987. *Beyond American Hegemony: The Future of the Western Alliance*. New York: Basic Books.

Capitanchik, David, and Richard C. Eichenberg. 1983. *Defense and Public Opinion*. Chatham House Papers 20. London: Routledge and Kegan Paul.

Carlucci, Frank. 1988. *Report on Allied Contributions to the Common Defense*. Washington, D.C.: Department of Defense.

Cauley, Jon, Todd Sandler, and Richard Cornes. 1986. "Nonmarket Institutional Structures: Conjectures, Distribution, and Allocative Efficiency." *Public Finance* 41:153–72.

Chapman, J. W. M., R. Drifte, and I. T. M. Gow. 1982. *Japan's Quest for Comprehensive Security: Defense—Diplomacy—Security*. New York: St. Martin's.

Cheney, Richard. (1989, 1990, 1991) *Report on Allied Contributions to the Common Defense*. Washington, D.C.: Department of Defense.

Cheung, Tai Ming, Susumu Awanohara, Shim Jae Hoon, and James Clad. 1990. "The New Disorder." *Far Eastern Economic Review* 13 December: 25–26.

Cohen, Benjamin J. 1977. *Organizing the World's Money: The Political Economy of International Monetary Relations*. New York: Basic Books.

Commission of the European Communities. *Eurobarometer* 32 (December): A41.

Congressional Record. 1984. Senate, 98th Cong., 2d sess. (20 June): 1–7.

Connolly, Michael. 1970. "Public Goods, Externalities, and International Relations." *Journal of Political Economy* 72:279–90.

———. 1972. "Trade in Public Goods: A Diagrammatic Analysis." *Quarterly Journal of Economics* 86:61–78.

———. 1976. "Optimal Trade in Public Goods." *Canadian Journal of Economics* 9:702–5.

Converse, Philip E. 1964. "The Nature of Belief Systems in Mass Publics." In *Ideology and Discontent,* edited by David E. Apter. New York: Free Press.

Cooper, Richard N. 1987. "Trade Policy as Foreign Policy." In *U.S. Trade Policies in a Changing World Economy,* edited by Robert M. Stein. Cambridge: MIT Press.

Cornes, Richard, and Todd Sandler. 1984a. "Easy Riders, Joint Production, and Public Goods." *Economic Journal* 94:580–98.

———. 1984b. "The Theory of Public Goods: Non-Nash Behavior." *Journal of Public Economics* 23:367–69.

Dobson, Wendy. 1991. *Economic Policy Coordination: Requiem or Prologue?* Washington, D.C.: Institute for International Economics.

Domke, William K., Richard C. Eichenberg, and Catherine M. Kelleher. 1987. "Consensus Lost? Domestic Politics and the 'Crisis' in NATO." *World Politics* 41:382–407.

Emminger, Otmar. 1977. "The Role of Monetary Policy Coordination to Attain Exchange-Rate System." In *The New International Monetary System,* edited by Robert A. Mundell and Jacques J. Polak. New York: Columbia University Press.

Eurogroup. 1988. *Western Defense: The European Role in NATO.* Brussels.

"Europe's Internal Market." 1989. *Economist,* 8 July.

Fitoussi, J.-P, and E. S. Phelps. 1986. "Causes of the 1980s Slump in Europe." *Brookings Papers on Economic Activity 1986:* 487–520.

Flanagan, Stephen J., and Keith A. Dunn. 1990. "NATO's Fifth Decade: Renewal or Midlife Crisis." In *NATO in the Fifth Decade,* edited by Stephen J. Flanagan and Keith A. Dunn. Washington, D.C.: National Defense University Press.

Flynn, Gregory. 1981. "Western Security in the 1980s: A Familiar European Context in a Changing World." In *The Internal Fabric of Western Security,* edited by Gregory Flynn et al. London: Allanheld, Osmun.

Flynn, Gregory, et al. 1981. *The Internal Fabric of Western Security.* London: Allanheld, Osmun.

Flynn, Gregory, and Hans Rattinger, eds. 1985. *The Public and Atlantic Defense.* London: Rowan and Allanheld.

Freedman, Lawrence, ed. 1983. *The Troubled Alliance: Atlantic Relations in the 1980s.* New York: St. Martin's.

Friedman, Thomas L. 1991. "NATO Tries to Ease Military Concern in Eastern Europe." *New York Times,* June 7.

Funabashi, Yoichi. 1989. *Managing the Dollar: From the Plaza to the Louvre,* 2d ed. Washington, D.C.: Institute for International Economics.

Gallup Organization. 1988. "Attitudes Toward U.S.-European Relations: A Report on American Public Opinion About Western Europe." Report GO87217. Washington, D.C.: Delegation of the Commission of the European Communities.

Gallup Political Index. 1980. *Report 238*. June. London: Gallup International Research Institute.

———. 1981. *Report 250*. June. London: Gallup International Research Institute.

———. 1982. *Report 259*. March. London: Gallup International Research Institute.

———. Various years. *Year End Survey*. London: Gallup International Research Institute.

Gilpin, Robert. 1987. *The Political Economy of International Relations*. Princeton: Princeton University Press.

Gowa, Joanne. 1989. "Rational Hegemons, Excludable Public Goods, and Small Groups: An Epitaph for Hegemonic Stability Theory." *World Politics* 41:307–24.

Haas, Ernst B. 1976. "Turbulent Fields and the Theory of Regional Integration." *International Organization* 30:173–212.

Hahn, Walter F., and Robert L. Pfaltzgraff, Jr., eds. 1979. *Atlantic Community in Crisis: A Redefinition of the Transatlantic Relationship*. New York: Pergamon.

Hansen, Laura, James C. Murdoch, and Todd Sandler. 1990. "On Distinguishing the Behavior of Nuclear and Non-Nuclear Allies in NATO." *Defence Economics* 1:37–56.

Hardin, Russell. 1982. "Collective Action as an Agreeable *n*- Prisoners' Dilemma." In *Rational Man and Irrational Society? An Introduction and Sourcebook*, edited by Brian Barry and Russel Hardin. Beverly Hills: Sage.

Harris Survey. 1985. "Public Wants Western Europe, Japan More Open to US Trade." Press Release 75, 16 September.

Hastings, Elizabeth Hann, and Philip K. Hastings. 1986, 1987, 1988, 1989, 1990. *Index to International Public Opinion*. New York: Greenwood.

Head, John G., and Carl S. Shoup. 1969. "Public Goods, Private Goods, and Ambiguous Goods." *Economic Journal* 79:576–72.

———. 1973. "Public Goods, Private Goods, and Ambiguous Goods Reconsidered." *Public Finance* 28:384–92.

Hoag, Malcolm W. 1967. "Increasing Returns in Military Production Functions." In *Issues in Defense Economics*, edited by Roland N. McKean. New York: Columbia University Press.

Hoekman, Bernard M. 1989. "Determining the Need for Issue Linkages in Multilateral Trade Negotiations," *International Organization* 43:693–714.

Holm-Pedersen, Helene. 1990. "Non-Military Cooperation in the North Atlantic Treaty Organization. Masters thesis, University of Connecticut.

Ikenberry, G. John, and Charles A. Kupchan. 1990. "Socialization and Hegemonic Power." *International Organization* 44:283–315.

Ilgen, Thomas L. 1985. *Autonomy and Interdependence: U.S.-Western European and Trade Relations, 1958–1984*. Totowa, N.J.: Rowman and Allanheld.

Japanese Defense Agency. 1987. *Defense of Japan, 1987*. Tokyo.

Jones, Philip R. 1988. "Defense Alliances and International Trade." *Journal of Conflict Resolution* 32:123–40.

Katzenstein, Peter J. 1978. "Introduction: Domestic and International Forces and Strategies of Foreign Economic Policy." In *Between Power and Plenty:*

Foreign Economic Policies of Advanced Industrialized States, edited by Peter J. Katzenstein. Madison: University of Wisconsin Press.

Kennedy, Paul. 1987. *The Rise and Fall of the Great Powers.* New York: Random House.

Keohane, Robert O. 1984. *After Hegemony: Cooperation and Discord in the World Political Economy.* Princeton: Princeton University Press.

Keohane, Robert O., and Joseph S. Nye. 1977. *Power and Interdependence: World Politics in Transition.* Boston: Little, Brown.

Kiesling, Herbert J. 1972. *The Possibilities for Trade in Public Goods in a System of Local Governments.* Working Paper 1207–17. Washington, D.C.: Urban Institute.

———. 1974. "Public Goods and the Possibilities for Trade." *Canadian Journal of Economics* 7:402–17.

Kindleberger, Charles P. 1973. *The World Economy in Depression, 1929–1939.* Berkeley and Los Angeles: University of California Press.

———. 1976. "Systems of International Economic Organization." In *Money and the Coming World Order,* edited by David P. Calleo. New York: New York University Press.

———. 1981. "Dominance and Leadership in the International Economy." *International Studies Quarterly* 25:242–54.

———. 1986. "Hierarchy versus International Cooperation." *International Organization* 40:841–47.

Kirkpatrick, Jeane J. 1990. "Beyond the Cold War." *Foreign Affairs (America and the World 1989/90,* 69:1–16.

Klosko, George. 1990. "The Obligation to Contribute to Discretionary Public Goods." *Political Studies* 38:196–214.

Knorr, Klaus. 1977. "Economic Interdependence and National Security." In *Economic Issues and National Security,* edited by Klaus Knorr and Frank N. Trager. Lawrence: Regents Press of Kansas.

———. 1985. "Burden-Sharing in NATO: Aspects of U.S. Policy." *Orbis* (Fall): 517–36.

Kondracke, Morton. 1990. "Who Needs NATO? *New Republic* (5 March): 14–15.

Krause, Lawrence B. 1968. *European Economic Integration and the United States.* Washington, D.C.: Brookings.

Kudrle, Robert T., and Davis B. Bobrow. 1991. "The G-7 After Hegemony: Compatibility, Cooperation and Conflict." In *World Leadership and Hegemony,* edited by David P. Rapkin. Boulder: Lynne Reinner.

Lake, David A. 1983. "International Economic Structures and American Foreign Policy, 1887–1934." *World Politics* 36:517–43.

Loehr, William. 1973. "Collective Goods and International Cooperation: Comments." *International Organization* 27:421–30.

Lowenthal, Abraham F. 1987. "Rethinking U.S. Interests in the Western Hemisphere." *Journal of InterAmerican Studies and World Affairs* 29:1–23.

Luce, R. Duncan, and Howard Raiffa. 1957. *Games and Decisions: Introduction and Critical Survey.* New York: John Wiley and Sons.

McGinnis, Michael D. 1986. "Issue Linkage and the Evolution of Cooperation." *Journal of Conflict Resolution* 30:141–70.

McGuire, Martin, and C. H. Groth, Jr. 1985. "A Method for Identifying the Public Good Allocation Process within a Group." *Quarterly Journal of Economics* 100:915–34.

Madison, Christopher. 1983. "At the Summit—Avoiding Disagreements Can Sometimes Spell Genuine Victory." *National Journal.* June 4.

Maroni, Alice C., and John J. Ulrich. 1985. *The U.S. Commitment to Europe's Defense: A Review of Costs Issues and Estimates.* Report 85-211 F. Washington, D.C.: Congressional Research Service.

Marris, Stephen. 1987. *Deficits and the Dollar: The World Economy at Risk,* rev. ed. Washington, D.C.: Institute for International Economics.

Marsh, Catherine, and Colin Fraser. 1989. "Nuclear Issues and the Nature of Public Opinion." In *Public Opinion and Nuclear Weapons,* edited by Catherine Marsh and Colin Fraser. London: Macmillan.

Martilla, John. 1989. "American Public Opinion: Evolving Definitions of National Security." In *America's Global Interests: A New Agenda,* edited by Edward K. Hamilton. New York: Norton.

Marwell, Gerald, and Ruth E. Ames. 1979. "Experiments on the Provision of Public Goods I: Resources, Interest, Group Size, and the Free Rider Problem." *American Journal of Sociology* 84:1335–60.

———. 1980. "Experiments on the Provision of Public Goods II: Provision Points, Stakes, Experience, and the Free Rider Problem." *American Journal of Sociology* 85:926–37.

———. 1981. "Economists Free Ride, Does Anyone Else? Experiments on the Provision of Public Goods IV." *Journal of Public Economics* 15:311–36.

Matthews, Jessica Tuchman. 1989. "Redefining Security." *Foreign Affairs* 68:162–77.

Mearsheimer, John J. 1990a. "Why We Will Soon Miss the Cold War." *Atlantic Monthly* (August 1990). 35–50.

———. 1990b. "Back to the Future: Instability in Europe after the Cold War." *International Security* 15:5–56.

Miller, Nicholas R. 1977. " 'Social Preference' and Game Theory: A Comment on 'The Dilemma of a Paretian Liberal.' " *Public Choice* 30:23–28.

Morrison, Denton E., and Ramon E. Henkel. 1970. "Significance Tests Reconsidered." In *The Significance Test Controversy: A Reader,* edited by Denton E. Morrison and Ramon E. Henkel. Chicago: Aldine.

Murdoch, James C., and Todd Sandler. 1982. "A Theoretical and Empirical Analysis of NATO." *Journal of Conflict Resolution* 26:237–63.

———. 1984. "Complementarity, Free-Riding, and the Military Expenditures of NATO Allies." *Journal of Public Economics* 25:83–101.

National Opinion Research Center. 1991. *General Social Survey.* Storrs: University of Connecticut, Roper Center Archives.

NATO (North Atlantic Treaty Organization). 1990. *London Declaration on a Transformed North Atlantic Alliance.* Brussels: NATO Information Service.

Nau, Henry R. 1990. *The Myth of America's Decline: Leading the World Economy in the 1990s.* New York: Oxford University Press.

Nelson, Daniel N., and Joseph Lepgold. 1986. "Alliances and Burden-Sharing: A NATO-Warsaw Pact Comparison." *Defense Analysis* 2:205–24.

Nye, Joseph S., Jr. 1990. *Bound to Lead: The Changing Nature of American Power.* New York: Basic Books.

Oakland, William H. 1969. "Joint Goods." *Economica* 36:253–68.

———. 1972. "Congestion, Public Goods, and Welfare." *Journal of Public Economics* 1:339–57.

Odell, John S. 1982. *U.S. International Monetary Policy: Markets, Power, and Ideas as Sources of Change.* Princeton: Princeton University Press.

OECD (Organization for Economic Cooperation and Development). 1984, 1985. *Science and Technology Indicators, Basic Statistical Series.* Vol. B, Gross National Expenditure on R&D. Paris: OECD.

———. 1985. *Geographical Distributions of Financial Flows to Developing Countries.* Paris: OECD.

———. 1987. *National Accounts: Main Aggregates.* Vol. 1, *1960–1985.* Paris: OECD.

———. Various years. *Development Cooperation.* Paris: OECD.

Olson, Mancur. 1965. *The Logic of Collective Action: Public Goods and the Theory of Groups.* Cambridge: Harvard University Press.

Olson, Mancur, and Richard Zeckhauser. 1966. "An Economic Theory of Alliances." *Review of Economics and Statistics* 48:266–79.

———. 1967. "Collective Goods, Comparative Advantage, and Alliance Efficiency." In *Issues in Defense Economics,* Roland N. McKean. New York: National Bureau of Economic Research.

———. 1970. "The Efficient Production of External Economies." *American Economic Review* 60:512–17.

Oneal, John R. 1990a. "The Theory of Collective Action and Burden Sharing in NATO." *International Organization* 44:379–402.

———. 1990b. "Testing the Theory of Collective Action: NATO Defense Burdens, 1950–1984." *Journal of Conflict Resolution* 34:426–48.

Oneal, John R., and Paul Diehl. 1990. "The Theory of Collective Action and NATO Defense Burdens." Unpublished paper.

Oneal, John R., and Mark A. Elrod. 1989. "NATO Burden-Sharing and the Forces of Change." *International Studies Quarterly.*

"Opinion Roundup." 1989. *Public Opinion* (March–April): 21–33 and (May–June): 21–29.

Oppenheimer, Joe. 1979. "Collective Goods and Alliances: A Reassessment." *Journal of Conflict Resolution* 23:387–407.

Oye, Kenneth A., ed. 1986. *Cooperation under Anarchy.* Princeton: Princeton University Press.

Oye, Kenneth A. 1979. "The Domain of Choice," edited by Kenneth A. Oye, Donald Rothchild and Robert Lieber. *Eagle Entangled.* New York: Longman.

Palmer, Glenn. 1989. "Collective Goods, Might, and Commitment: Contribution of Mechanisms in NATO." Paper presented at the annual meetings of the American Political Science Association, August 31–September 3, Atlanta.

———. 1990. "Corralling the Free-Rider: Deterrence and the Western Alliance." *International Studies Quarterly* 34:147–64.

Pauly, Mark V. 1970. "Optimality, 'Public' Goods, and Local Governments: A General Theoretical Analysis." *Journal of Political Economy* 78:572–85.

Payne, Rodger A. 1990. "The Social Dimension of Nuclear Deterrence Strategy." Unpublished paper.

Pick, Hella. 1990. "NATO Faces Identity Crisis in Tomorrow's Europe." *Guardian,* 20 September.

Pollard, Robert A. 1985. *Economic Security and the Origins of the Cold War, 1945–1950.* New York: Columbia University Press.

Prins, Gwyn. 1989. "How Change Became a Possibility." In *Public Opinion and Nuclear Weapons,* edited by Catherine Marsh and Colin Fraser. London: Macmillan.

Putnam, Robert D. 1988. "Diplomacy and Domestic Politics: The Logic of Two-Level Games." *International Organization* 42:427–60.

Putnam, Robert D., and Nicholas Bayne. 1984. *Hanging Together: The Seven-Power Summits.* Cambridge: Harvard University Press.

Raiffa, Howard. 1982. *The Art and Science of Negotiation.* Cambridge: Harvard University Press.

Riding, Alan. 1990. "NATO Struggling to Redefine Itself." *New York Times,* 24 September.

Rowen, Hobart. 1987. "Finance Heads Agree to Stop Dollar's Fall: Leading Industrial Nations Vow Cooperation." *Washington Post,* 23 February.

Russett, Bruce. 1970. *What Price Vigilance? The Burdens of National Defense.* New Haven: Yale University Press.

———. 1985. "The Mysterious Case of Vanishing Hegemony; or, Is Mark Twain Really Dead?" *International Organization* 39:207–31.

Safire, William. 1988. "The European Pillar." *New York Times,* 7 April.

Samuelson, Paul. 1954. "The Pure Theory of Public Expenditure." *Review of Economics and Statistics* 36:387–89.

Sandler, Todd. 1977. "Impurity of Defense: An Application to the Economics of Alliances." *Kyklos* 30:443–60.

Sandler, Todd, and Jon Cauley. 1975. "On the Economic Theory of Alliances." *Journal of Conflict Resolution* 19:330–348.

———. 1977. "The Design of Supranational Organizations." *International Studies Quarterly* 21:251–76.

Sandler, Todd, Jon Cauley, and John F. Forbes. 1980. "In Defense of a Collective Goods Theory of Alliances." *Journal of Conflict Resolution* 24:537–47.

Sandler, Todd, and John F. Forbes. 1980. "Burden-Sharing, Strategy, and the Design of NATO." *Economic Inquiry* 18:425–44.

Sandler, Todd, and James Murdoch. 1990. "Nash-Cournot or Lindahl Behavior? An Empirical Test for the NATO Allies." *Quarterly Journal of Economics* 105:875–94.

Satoh, Yukio. 1982. *The Evolution of Japanese Security Policy.* Adelphi Paper 178. London: International Institute of Strategic Studies.

Scherr, B., and E. Babb. 1975. "Pricing Public Goods: An Experiment with Two Proposed Pricing Systems." *Public Choice* 23:35–48.

Schmidt, Helmut. 1978. "The 1977 Alastair Buchan Memorial Lecture." *Survival* 20:2–10.

Sebenius, James K. 1983. "Negotiation Arithmetic: Adding and Subtracting Issues and Parties." *International Organization* 37:281–316.

———. 1984. *Negotiating the Law of the Sea.* Cambridge: Harvard University Press.

Sen, Amartya. 1970. "The Impossibility of a Paretian Liberal." *Journal of Political Economy* 78:152–57.

Sherwood, Elizabeth. 1990. *Allies in Crisis*. New Haven: Yale University Press.

Siegel, Sidney. 1956. *Nonparametric Statistics for the Behavioral Sciences*. New York: McGraw-Hill.

SIPRI (Stockholm International Peace Research Institute). Various years. *SIPRI Yearbook of World Armaments and Disarmaments*. Oxford: Oxford University Press.

Sloan, Stanley R. 1985a. *Defense Burden-Sharing: U.S. Relations with the NATO Allies and Japan*. 85-101 F. Washington, D.C.: Congressional Research Service.

———. 1985b. *NATO's Future: Toward a New Transatlantic Bargain*. Washington, D.C.: National Defense University Press.

———. 1987. "The Political Dynamics of Defense Burden-Sharing in NATO." In *Evolving European Defense Policies*, edited by Catherine M. Kelleher and Gale A. Mattox. Lexington: Lexington Books.

———. 1990. "NATO's Future in a New Europe: An American Perspective." *International Affairs* 63:495–511.

Smith, Steven K., and Douglas A. Wertman. 1989. "Summing up before the Economic Summit." *Public Opinion*. (March–April): 41–45.

Snidal, Duncan. 1985. "The Limits of Hegemonic Stability Theory." *International Organization* 39:579–614.

Snyder, Glenn H. 11961. *Deterrence and Defense: Toward a Theory of National Security*. Princeton: Princeton University Press.

Solomon, Robert. 1982. *The International Monetary System, 1945–1981*, rev. ed. New York: Harper and Row.

Starr, Harvey. 1974. "A Collective Goods Analysis of the Warsaw Pact after Czechoslovakia." *International Organization* 28:521–32.

Starrels, John. 1989. "At Last, Japan Takes Center Stage." *New York Times*, 16 July.

Steel, Ronald. 1990. "Europe after the Superpowers." In *Sea Changes: American Foreign Policy in a Transformed World*, edited by Nicholas X. Rizopoulos. New York: Council on Foreign Relations Press.

Stein, Arthur A. 1980. "The Politics of Linkage." *World Politics* 33:62–81.

Strange, Susan. 1987. "The Persistent Myth of Lost Hegemony." *International Organization* 41:551–74.

———. 1990. "The Name of the Game." In *Sea Changes: American Foreign Policy in a Transformed World*, edited by Nicholas X. Rizopoulos. New York: Council on Foreign Relations Press.

Sullivan, Leonard. 1985. "A New Approach to Burden Sharing." *Foreign Policy* 60:91–110.

Sweeney, J. 1973. "An Experimental Investigation of the Free Rider Problem." *Social Science Research* 2:277–92.

Taylor, Michael. 1976. *Anarchy and Cooperation*. London: John Wiley and Sons.

Theis, Wallace. 1989. "Crises and the Study of Alliance Politics." *Armed Forces and Society* 15:349–69.

Tollison, Robert D., and Thomas D. Willett. 1976. "Institutional Mechanisms for Dealing with International Externalities: A Public Choice Perspective." In *The Law of the Sea: U.S. Interests and Alternatives*, edited by Ryan

C. Amacher and Richard James Sweeney. Washington, D.C.: American Enterprise Institute.

————. 1979. "An Economic Theory of Mutually Advantageous Issue Linkages in International Negotiations." *International Organization* 33:425–49.

Tsebelis, George. 1990. *Nested Games: Rational Choice in Comparative Politics.* Berkeley and Los Angeles: University of California Press.

Ullman, Richard. 1983. "Redefining Security." *International Security* 8:129–53.

UNESCO (U.N. Educational, Scientific, and Cultural Organization). Various years. *UNESCO Statistical Yearbook.* New York: UNESCO.

U.S. Department of Defense. 1989. *The Secretary's Report to Congress.* Washington, D.C.: Department of Defense.

U.S. Department of State. 1989. *The NATO Summit: 40 Years of Success.* Selected Document 37. Washington, D.C.: Department of State, Bureau of Public Affairs.

U.S. House of Representatives. 1987. *Challenges to NATO's Consensus: West European Attitudes and U.S. Policy.* Report prepared for the subcommittee on Europe and Middle East of the Committee on Foreign Affairs. Washington, D.C.: Government Printing Office.

U.S. Information Agency. 1984. *NATO and Burden-Sharing.* Research Report R-11-84. Washington, D.C.: U.S. Information Agency.

U.S. International Communication Agency. 1982. *West European Public Opinion on Security Issues, 1981–1982.* Research Report R-10-82. Washington, D.C.: U.S. International Communication Agency.

Vatikiotis, Michael. 1990. "Yankee Please Stay." *Far Eastern Economic Review.* 13 December.

Wagner, R. Harrison. 1983. "The Theory of Games and the Problem of International Cooperation." *American Political Science Review* 77:330–46.

Wallace, William. 1976. "Atlantic Relations: Policy Coordination and Conflict." *International Affairs* 52:163–79.

Walt, Stephen. 1987. *The Origins of Alliances.* Ithaca: Cornell University Press.

Waltz, Kenneth. 1979. *Theory of International Politics.* Reading, Mass.: Addison-Wesley.

Wegener, Henning. 1989. "The Management of Change: NATO's Anniversary Summit." *NATO Review* 37:1–7.

Weisman, Steven R. 1984. "Seven Leaders Declare Political Values at Economic Talks." *New York Times,* 6 June.

Wendt, Allan. 1990. *A Restructured COCOM.* Current Policy Paper 1290. Washington, D.C.: Department of State.

Wightman, David. Forthcoming. "The Bretton Woods System and the Return to Dollar Convertibility in Europe." *Rivista di Storia Economica.* 9.

Williamson, John. 1977. *The Failure of World Monetary Reform, 1971–1974.* New York: New York University Press.

Wolfe, Robert. 1990–91. "Atlanticism without the Wall: Transatlantic Co-Operation and the Transformation of Europe." *International Journal* 46:137–63.

Yasatumo, Dennis T. 1986. *The Manner of Giving: Strategic Aid and Japanese Foreign Policy.* Lexington, Mass.: Lexington Books.

Ypersele de Strihou, J. 1967. "Sharing the Defense Burden among Western Allies." *Review of Economics and Statistics* 49:527–36.

Index

171

Designed by Bruce Gore
Composed by WorldComp
in Baskerville
Printed by Princeton University Press
50-lb. Glatfelter Offset, B-16, and bound in ICG Arrestox A 51500,
    stamped with S43 Copperfoil by General Roll Leaf.
    Head and foot bands in green and white.